Live Like You Give A Fuck

Create the Life You Want NOW...
Not Later

Nicola Findlay

Clink
Street

London | New York

Published by Clink Street Publishing 2017

Copyright © 2017

First edition.

ISBN:
978-1-912262-23-6 paperback
978-1-912262-24-3 ebook

To all the wonder women in my life especially Melia.

And to all the beautiful woman reading this book: step up, shake your ass and do your 'thang'

Author Bio

Nicola Findlay has worked with hundreds of people in personal development workshops and corporate training to smash it in life and business.

Nicola lives in Surrey, England and is Mama to Melia. She loves doing work she gives a fuck about, travelling to the sun and frequently enjoys a chilled glass of prosecco while planning and plotting her next adventure.

Contents

Introduction

You spoilt bitch.

There are people who are suffering in this crazy fucked-up world with no food, water, shelter or safety, just some of the basic human needs required to survive.

Yet, in wealthy, Western, capitalistic societies we believe life sucks because we can't connect to wifi, the queue for a skinny latte is out the door and the daily commute takes longer than watching the latest box set of *Game of Thrones*. #bullshitfirstworldproblems.

We really are bunch of selfish, spoilt brats. Those who are really suffering, would kill to have our problems. Would you trade places with a refugee? No, didn't think so.

We are so rich and wealthy beyond belief but we don't often take the time to realise it. We can run a tap and get water in an instant. Where exactly has it come from? Who cares, when we need it, it's there and we don't have to go on a five-mile trek to get it. So let's just appreciate the fuck out of that. You can sit in comfort, on your couch, in your pyjamas and order pretty much anything you want online. From groceries, clothing, make up, furniture; and a lot of this stuff will arrive the very next day. It's like a modern day miracle, we love you Amazon Prime.

And, one of my favourites. You can buy a ticket that enables you to fly... in the sky, where we can't naturally breathe, above the clouds, to another fucking country, and get there in a matter of hours. This shit is incredible but what do we chose to focus on? Moaning our asses off about the queue at passport control or how long it took to collect the hold luggage. We forget to breathe in the pure magic of taking flight. For some people modern life sucks; to me it's a fucking miracle. The greatest Kings and Queens from history would've given all of their riches to experience the modern luxuries that today we take for granted.

We live in this miracle of a world yet I see way too many people giving up on their dreams. It's like they got a memo saying they can come and do this crazy thing called life again, so they're using this lifetime as a dress rehearsal. It's all too easy to get stuck on the merry-go-round of life where you seem to be in a perpetual groundhog day, doing the same shit over and over again. Wake up, get ready, go to your shit job, eat, sleep and fucking repeat. You see other people who've escaped the merry-go-around who are running wild and free. They're not stuck, they're loving the daily grind because it's the grind they created. And you're secretly wishing, hoping and wanting that to be you. But wait... it can be. What if you were unstoppable? What if there were no chains holding you back? What if you designed and lived your life exactly how you wanted it to be instead of praying that things will change?

Isn't it time to wake the fuck up and cut loose from a life you don't want to lead?

You deserve to be in the realms of making your one and only lifetime count and living a journey where fulfilment and satisfaction are completely off the scale.

This is why I designed the five 'accessories' that will make your outfit of life absolutely pop, this season and next. These accessories will work miracles for you and allow you to be the fiercest version of yourself. Not only that but these accessories are reusable timeless classics which are an investment for a lifetime and much cheaper than a Chanel boy bag.

These five simple accessories are the formula you need to really *live like you give a fuck* which is a fully blown, awesome and fulfilling life. I use the term fulfilment deliberately instead of success. When the word 'success' is used it often conjures up the image of financial and material success and this alone is not what we're looking for here people. Of course, that dream house, car, holidays, clothes and whatever other material bullshit you want is nice, but you can still have all of that crap and not be happy. We've seen enough A-listers in rehab to know that. The crucial thing to understand is that none of that shit matters if you don't have an emotionally wealthy bank account, if you don't know how to appreciate what you've already got and if you don't love yourself.

What we're looking for is a feeling, a truth and most importantly your growth. A cultivation of gratefulness and a certainty in yourself that you are on a mission to hound your passions and purposes in life. That's when you wake up and before your eyelids have even cracked open you feel as lucky as fuck. Don't get me wrong, I'm not expecting you to see fluffy unicorns dancing across a rainbow. Just a sure, realistic sense that you are making your precious time on this planet count and loving your sexy self every... single... day. Who the hell doesn't want a dose of that? And this shit is legal.

Right now, I am not your coach, I'm not the author of your destiny. I'm that raging voice inside your head who is desperate to see what you're capable of achieving in this lifetime, not the next. I want you to strut through life kicking down the doors that you want to open, even in your heels.

I'll be honest with you there's no rocket science, cure for cancer or some big secret that nobody told you included here. What you will find is a lot of common sense and practical exercises so that you can start the ignition and power up that beautiful engine of yours... vroom vroom... and I for one can't wait to see you purr.

We are all unique individuals who get motivated and inspired in a huge range of different ways. So, don't see this as a bible that is set in stone. See it as guide and take what works for you and leave what doesn't, I won't be offended.

This is your life, and getting it right is not a 'one size fits all' approach. So, if you love some of the concepts go all in 100% with those and if you think others are crap then drop them like a sack of shit. I love that because:

a) you can manage your own mind

b) you're tuned into yourself

So roll with the goodies that work and feel natural for you.

I started my empowerment journey in my early twenties. I spent years reading the bibles of self-help books, while my mates were reading *OK* magazine. Did to death the weekend seminars where I walked across hot burning coals and karate chopped through wood to condition my mind to do anything, while my friends were partying. What a fool, but hey it worked. I've listened to old school-style audio tapes and I've watched shitloads of old guys in suits with their amazing philosophies, while others were watching TV. I've done the crack course in Neuro Linguistic Programming delivered personal coaching workshops and designed and delivered corporate training. And what I've realised through everything I've learnt and taught is that these philosophies are incredible and they work. That's why I want to share it with you, and do it in a way that's not going to bore your ass off.

Also, I don't want this book to be a waste of your time or mine because time is the most valuable commodity we own. I spent my precious time writing this book so that it makes a difference in your life, not just for it to look pretty on your bookshelf. So, to stop that from happening, practical and meaningful exercises are included to stir the fire in your belly and imagination. But I'm going to need you to promise me something. That you'll be totally honest with yourself, so that you get the most out of this. It's not a test, no one's going to come and mark your answers. As long as your answers are intuitive and from the heart they'll all be 100% right. So, no cheating, just pull up your big girl panties, or sexy thong for that matter, do the work and start relishing in your results. You may want to keep tissues handy for some of the exercises.

4

The Universe at Play

Through time, study and personal experience I've realised that there's something bigger than us at play. It's something that I've learnt to trust and get fully aligned with. It's my number one BFF, I call her The Universe.

Before you get all weirded out, I haven't turned into a spiritual hippie, it's just the basic laws of quantum physics, which are fact. Every single thing on this planet when broken down into its most microscopic form is energy. And energy, like high-school kids, likes hanging around with other energy like itself. So positive waves of energy will flow and attract to other molecules of positive energy. And likewise, yup you guessed it, negative energy will attract to other forms of negative energy, which is commonly referred to as the Law of Attraction. The subject was written about back in the day as early as 1937 by Napoleon Hill in one of my favourite books *Think and Grow Rich* and more recently by Rhonda Byrne in the hugely successful book *The Secret.* Some people pooh pooh the idea but I've had too many examples of this force doing great things in my life to ignore it.

You might have your own name for this energy and call it God, the spirit, divine wisdom, call it bloody hocus pocus if you want, but please just understand the more you get in alignment with The Universe, and allow it to guide you to the things you want, you will be super surprised that it's real and it works.

Have you ever had a coincidence? Well girlfriend, there is no such thing. That is The Universe at play right there. Acknowledge it, be thankful for it and wait for more of that good energy to show up. When The Universe is at play and things happen that I can't explain or believe, I say that it's The Universe giving me a road-sign and I get super excited. The more you trust and believe in it, the harder it will work with you and the better life will get. The only condition I do believe you've got to sign up to is that you've got to get your ass into gear with action for the Law of Attraction to be of benefit to you. If you just lay back and wait for the perfect guy, job or home to fall into your lazy lap it won't happen. You've got to put some skin in the game to aid the manifestation process.

"Everything is energy and that's all there is to it. Match the frequency of the reality you want and you cannot help but get that reality. It can be no other way. This is not philosophy. This is Physics."

Albert Einstein

Steve Jobs once said: "You need to make a dent in the universe, otherwise why else be here?" So right now, for me, this book, my labour of love is me making my dent in The Universe and if this dent motivates, inspires or encourages even just one of you beautiful badass women out there in the world I'll be happier than a fat kid with cake.

So, What the Heck are You Doing Here?

You didn't just stumble across this book. The powers at play slapped this book in your face for a good reason. I'm no Einstein but I'm guessing that something is adrift in your life, or you are seeking something which you haven't yet found, or my favourite, you just want to ramp up the volume and start living life like a 'playing-full-out-mother-fucker'. Any one of these reasons is brilliant. There is a specific reason why these pages found their way to you. It could be that one line, one idea, one thought or habit you make blows your mind and makes a shift in a huge way for you.

Perhaps your boss is an asshole and makes your working life a living nightmare so you want to find a way to get the hell out of that office and start your own business. Maybe you absolutely love what you do but are dead-beat broke. Or perhaps it could be time to get rid of that bum in your life and find someone who deserves and appreciates you.

Or maybe, just maybe, your situation is not as extreme as that but you are in the worst situation of them all. You are in a perpetual groundhog day. Where everything is just OK, fine, hunky-dory and you're sat there thinking, is this it? R E A L L Y ? This is my life and I'm going to check out without ever really smashing it. So you're sort of, kind of hoping and praying for a bit of magic in your boring, average, unimaginative, repetitive life. You may have awesomeness sprinkled in with fun nights out here and there, or when you book or go on holiday. But are you truly waking up every single fucking day excited to be alive and kicking on this planet and driving full speed into your dreams? Or is everything just OK? I'm telling you; 'just OK' is a scary place to be, because if something is bad, fucked up or wrong, you know it's bad, fucked up or wrong. When you have enough leverage you will damn well do something about it, and when you do, that is where the magic truly happens. But when everything is OK, there is no reason for you to change anything in your life. You continue to coast along in neutral gear, where you only enjoy your days off, hate your boss, wish your partner would get their act together, where you think the life you want is for someone else. Do you really want to live a life of OK? I'll answer that for you... Fuck No!!

Some people are meant to live a more subdued life, with less thrills and spills and that suits them just fine. They are happy without a purpose or a passion, they prefer to glide through life, shrug their shoulders and just see what happens, and we shouldn't force the notion that you have to have some huge mission or purpose in life onto people. However, the fact that you are reading this fucking book tells us that you know you are destined for something greater in life than OK.

Who the hell wants to live a life of OK, of mediocrity, of 'fine'? Come on, let's live a little! There's no spark, or fun, or challenge, or passion, or growth in OK!! There's no awesomeness or 'outstandingness' in OK. OK is settling for a life of second best, and you know it. Take your bad self to the next level and live a life of more than mediocrity:

- because you know you're not 100% fulfilled where you are
- because you owe it to yourself to find out the woman you are capable of becoming
- because you'll learn and grow along the journey
- because you'll inspire not only yourself but others around you too
- because you'll experience adventures, travel, friendships and loves that you never could have imagined
- because you are going to fucking LOVE IT when you get there

"Normal is nothing to aspire to, it's something to get away from."

Jodie Foster – Actress

The author Stephen Covey said in his brilliant book *The 7 Habits of Highly Effective People* that we should start with the end in mind. The guy literally meant that we should take a moment and focus on the end of our lives, as in, when we are dead! When I first read this, I was like; 'What is this guy on?', as it sounded a bit morbid, but stick with it because he was onto a winner. The idea was to focus specifically on your funeral and have time to reflect on your life and what the hell you've been doing on this planet. If you continue on your current course will it have been meaningful, impactful and fulfilling to you? Would you have had those crazy adventures, tried those new things, read those books, travelled afar and had the experiences that would have made life mesmerising? It's also a great idea to think about who would be in attendance at your funeral and what they would say about you – all marvellous things I'm sure. I think it's a brilliant exercise because when it's all said and done you need to know why the fuck you were here. What do you want people to say about you when you've gone? How do you want them to feel about you? More importantly how did you make others feel? What legacy do you want to leave behind? How did you help or change people's lives? What did you do when you had life that made it count? If you don't know the answer right now, don't worry we have much work to do on this later but just know that whatever it is, it is possible for you.

The very fact that you were able to open your eyes this morning means you're lucky. You get another VIP day pass on this planet when many who were here yesterday didn't. All the years you've survived on this planet you've managed to dodge the bullets of death coming at you from ill-health, tragic accidents, natural disasters and psychotic terrorists. You're still here so... *Live Like You Give A Fuck.*

"Life may not be perfect, but at least you have one."

This may sound cringey but just think, over 100 million sperm swam up your mother's vagina – yeah I really did just say that. And these hard-core soldiers battled it out in her fallopian tubes. This was like war, where only the fittest survived. Millions of sperm died on the journey to that sacred egg. But there was one determined little motherfucker out there who was like, I've got this, the prize is mine. He was the fittest, the strongest, the fastest and the smartest, he stayed alive and he won that race. He was the best of the best, the navy seal of sperm and you know what? He created YOU. All those other sperms would have created someone else so don't you see... YOU are a freakin' miracle!! After all that hard work facing death and beating 100 million others in the ultimate race he gets to see you sit around on your weary ass not living life at 100% because what? You're fearful, or worried about what others think of you, or you're scared of failure, or you're just plain old lazy, well boo fucking hoo! Guess what, those excuses aren't allowed here anymore!

My mother always knew that she only ever wanted to have two children. My older sister came along early in life for her and then a while later my mum and dad started trying for their second baby. Unfortunately, it wasn't plain sailing and my mother went through hell and endured the agony of a miscarriage at 14 weeks. Once she had physically recovered, my parents remained optimistic and starting trying to conceive again. The emotional scars were not so easy to heal though, especially as they had found out it was a little baby boy that mum had been carrying. I know that to this day mum has never forgotten about him. Mum was obviously a nervous wreck when she fell pregnant again but the doctors kept a closer eye on her and she had plenty of scans, and was indescribably relieved when she got the A-OK at 12 weeks. Mum had a very healthy pregnancy and had enjoyed getting the nursery and clothing ready for this little girl who was about to join the family. She was excited to go into the hospital when she started feeling the pangs of labour and called my dad to get his ass to the hospital quick time. While mum was in the hospital, really shitty complications arose and when the nurse checked for the baby's heartbeat it had disappeared and she gave my mother the most devastating news she would ever receive in her lifetime. Her full-term, unborn baby girl had died. My mother then had to go through the heart wrenching agony of going through labour to give birth to a stillborn baby.

When I was full-term in my pregnancy I thought about what my mother had gone through and imagined how I would have felt if I had lost my baby at that same point in time, but I couldn't and no one else could unless they've experienced it. You could never get anywhere close to imagining that kind of pain and torture. But my Mum was a damn strong woman and she didn't let that horrendous experience stop her from having her two children. So remarkably she tried yet again, and no fucking shit she had a perfectly healthy pregnancy and labour and she got... me! Albeit six weeks early, I wanted to keep them on their toes from the get-go. After a quick stint in the recovery unit I was good to go. Because of the distressing circumstances in which I came into the world I often have to reflect on why the hell this shit happened. Why the fuck did my mum have to go through all of that hurt and pain? I wouldn't wish that on my worst enemy and sometimes I feel a little guilty. Why is it that those two poor babies died and I didn't? My mother's stillborn baby, my sister Tara, is buried in Gibraltar and would have been two years older than me. What kind of sick joke is it that she is there, two feet under and I am here alive and kicking? This is why I can't take what we call LIFE for granted. My mum only ever wanted two children so if either of those two babies had survived I would not be here. So in a sense I feel like I was destined to be here – here for a reason, and I'm so grateful for my place. I want to make my time here count for something as so much was sacrificed for my place on this planet.

So I'm gonna live life full out like a crazy chick and do all the things I fucking love, and I'm going to do them now. Not when I'm 40 years old, not when I 'think' I'm more experienced, not when my child is older or has left home, not when I have more time or more money or when I've lost half a stone, I'm going to do that shit NOW, before the meter on my clock runs out and you know what, I suggest you do the fucking same.

So, I'm going to write this book
I'm going to run
I'm going to give my time to someone in need
I'm going to sunny climes frequently
I'm going to do yoga daily
I'm gonna deadlift 100 kilos
I'm going help people change their lives
I'm going to build a house
I'm going to love passionately
I'm going to live in my dream house
I'm going to have hard-core abs
I'm going to jump out of a plane
I'm going to raise money for charity
I'm going to love like a teenager
I'm going to travel in style
I'm going to empower women
I'm going to dress up, not down
I'm going to meditate
I'm going to listen to loud music daily
I'm going to leave people feeling more uplifted
I'm going to light the expensive candles any day of the week
I'm going to fuel my body respectfully
I'm going to dance in the kitchen and in the club
I'm going to drink champagne whenever the mood takes me
I'm going to spread my magic and love about this planet
And most of all I'm going to love me
And that's just for starters…

"Life is so damn short. For fuck's sake, just do what makes you happy."

Bill Murray

So What the Hell Do You Want?

Find a peaceful spot and keep asking yourself this question again, and again, and answer intuitively. Don't think hard about this. It may have been a while since you've paused time – time to reflect and think about what you want, so use this first exercise as a warm up. It doesn't have to be perfect, just brainstorm some of the things that you'd love to do.

Some things on your list may be much more achievable than others. You may have some silly things that are fun, like learning to hula hoop for one minute and something else that would be life-changing, like moving abroad. Don't waste time thinking about how you're going to accomplish it all with time or money etc, just let it all flow and damn well write it down, and we'll work on that detailed stuff later. This is getting you into the practice of consistently setting yourself some kick-ass positive intentions. The kind of stuff that just lights you up.

Time to get to work.
Start each sentence with I'm going to '.......' and complete the blanks.

_____

_____

_____

_____

_____

_____

_____

If you're struggling for ideas think about these ideas as inspiration; – where do I want to travel to, what adventures do I want to have, where would I love to live, what restaurants, do I want to eat at, what new things do I want to see, what experiences would I like to have, what new things do I want to try, what fear can I overcome, what do I want to study, what skill do I want to learn, what do I want to build, what do I want to make, what do I want to do because it's fun.

It's time you get your act together before it's too late, because nothing in life is guaranteed, well except death and taxes. Seriously every fucking day you are a little bit closer to dying so why the fuck aren't you jumping out of bed like your ass is on fire and living the exact life that you want? If you are doing that already fabulous, put the book down, and get straight back to it. If not, get your shit together and decide what you want in life, then grow some balls, figuratively speaking of course, and go get it.

So, are we understood? You can't live an outstanding life by living in the OK zone, like I said, it's a dangerous place to be. That's where you end up in an uninspiring existence which is like a nightmare you can't wake up from. Just OK is where things aren't bad enough for you to change but good enough for you to not want to change. Just good enough is not good enough for you.

"Life can be something to survive or the ultimate prize"

This isn't going to be easy. So, you need to get real honest with me. How badly do you fucking want this?

Whatever you want in life, it's going to cost you, so you need to decide how much are you willing to pay for what you want? When it comes to the crunch how much do you really want this, or is it just a lazy lacklustre fantasy? Are you willing to get up an hour earlier each day to exercise? Are you willing to run in the cold, wind and rain to keep fit? Are you willing to fail over and over again until you get it right in your business? Are you willing to sacrifice nights out and cute outfits to save for your mission? Are you willing to skip the latest boxset on Netflix to study? Are you willing to take heat from the haters when things start going well? If the answer is no, you may as well go snuggle up to a crappy, boring, lame and mediocrity life right now and put this book down, because I didn't write my ass off for losers. But if the answer is 'Hell Yes' then I'm super crazy excited for you. I'm excited about the possibilities you've just opened up for yourself. The dreams that you are now prepared to make a reality, the shifts that you will make that will attract positivity and opportunity. So now you're finally ready to step into that arena and play ball I want to show you how you can truly create the rollercoaster life of your dreams.

If reading any of these pages gives you that buzz of energy to go after your dreams, ideas or inspirations, the efforts of writing this book will be priceless to me. And as we're having a tender moment, there won't be many, I'd like to ask you to be open to trust – trust of yourself, your path and the workings of The Universe. Some of the concepts may sound a bit crazy, but just roll with them. I was doubtful at first until things starting shifting, changing and manifesting for me and my clients and it blew my mind, more than ten lines of cocaine ever could, or so I'm guessing. Commit to giving it a shot, and I promise you'll be amazed.

"You only get one life, so ride it til' the wheels come off."

Lisa Nichols

What I'm attempting to do here is to cut the crap, and give you the core basics of self-help, or as I call them, 'creating a life that you never fucking dreamt was possible', that I've learnt along the way that will transform your life, if you want them to. These are the essential accessories that every woman should value more than a Yves Saint Laurent clutch and a pair of Louboutins put together.

Everyone's wants, desires, goals and dreams are different. Determine what your missions are in life and go after them like a crazy son of a bitch. Sometimes my main focus and mission is to write, sometimes it's to run, sometimes it's to volunteer, sometimes it's to inspire or motivate and sometimes it can be to look after myself. For many years it was time out to raise my daughter. And sometimes it's a mix of all of the above. I have created a lifestyle and way of living that makes me feel like a rock star. My family is consciously connected and on fire. I've created a business that I love and get so freakin' passionate about. I earn plenty of money to support the lifestyle I want. My health is the best it's ever been, I contribute my time weekly to charity so my sense of contribution is off the scale and I've got awesome travel trips blowin' up my diary. I only keep quality people around me that energise and inspire me and I prioritise self-care with exercise, massages and pampering, so I live like a queen. 'Success' is not defined by having a million dollars in the bank, but by creating an everyday life and existence that blows my own mind and keeps my cup of fulfilment filled to the brim. And by continually assessing my goals and the fun things I want to do I'm on course to bring even more of what I want into my life. So you get it, I have created my ideal life, have helped my clients do it and now I want you to do the same in whatever shape or form that looks like to you.

"You have to design and define your success."

American psychologist Abraham Maslow stated that after your basic and psychological needs are met - such as food and water, shelter, safety and secure relationships as identified in his five-tier hierarchy of needs (so I was awake in psychology class) – the top goal of human motivation is 'Self Actualization', which means achieving one's full potential through personal growth and discovering self-fulfilment. Which in normal language means; to be the fucking best that you can be, in whatever form that means for you.

Your greatest dream or desire might be to travel and explore hidden parts of the world, be a CEO, create a fashion line, build a house, set up a charitable foundation, quit your 9–5, move abroad, create a wild and adventurous upbringing for your kids or create a health movement. You get the point, whatever the fuck it is, it's completely different for everyone. It's about what makes YOU happy and fulfilled deep down in your gut and in your soul. I can't impress that upon you enough!! You need to understand that and install that in your mind like the latest app. It's not about making your parents, partner or your boss happy, or doing exactly what all of your friends are doing because you think you should. If you spend a lifetime trying to please others you're really just living a lie and you know it.

You have to set your own life course, and no one is going to care more about your dream than you. Respect other people's dreams but most importantly respect your own.

So, are you ready? Buckle up, Let's do this...

Accessory No 1 – Beliefs

You are what you think. The way you talk to yourself and the thoughts you have control your behaviours, habits and actions. Change up your thinking and cut the invisible puppet strings that shape you.

"It's what you choose to believe that makes you the person you are."

Karen Marie Moning

Limit Those Bullshit Beliefs

I'll be honest with you, this isn't the sexiest subject in the world but it's the most important one, so stick with it because it underlines everything you do.

Our assumptions, values and beliefs are the way we view and judge ourselves and other people which then informs our outlook on the world. Our unique outlook on the world then influences how we behave, think and act. Some of these influences will be positive and help you to grow while others will hold you back and inhibit you; these shitty ones are called limiting beliefs. We have personal beliefs about all the different areas of our own lives which usually start with words like I'm too young, old, I'm rubbish at, I can't, or I'm not. We also have global beliefs about everything outside of ourselves such as politics, money, work, relationships and pretty much anything else you can think of.

For example, as a child you were witness to your parents' marriage. And they may have had a happily ever after kind of relationship, or they shouted and screamed until they got divorced kind of relationship. What you witnessed in that time will have subconsciously influenced your current view of marriage which has now in adulthood become your belief.

The freaking scary thing is you're not consciously aware of your beliefs and you believe them to be true even if they're not, so watch out for your own #fakenews. Our beliefs are very subtle and are affecting how we deal with our grown up ass lives and often they just don't serve us well anymore.

Why do these beliefs even exist? During your formative years you adopted your perceptions, values and beliefs about the big wide world from your parents, carers, teachers, family and just about anyone who influenced you during that time.

Some of our childhood beliefs were designed to protect us; hands up who heard 'don't talk to strangers'? Yet others were based on our upbringings, social backgrounds and our carers' prejudices and beliefs about the world. The things they believed to be true. Some parents had beliefs that their children should be seen and not heard. If you grew up in that environment it may influence how you now behave as an adult, you just may not be conscious of it.

Many of my clients have subconscious values and beliefs about relationships, money, sex, what career they 'should' do, what they think they're good and bad at, but understanding this concept is the first step in cutting this crap out of your life and creating awesome beliefs that will work with you not against you.

"Knock out your limiting beliefs before they take you in the next round."

Think of a limiting belief like a nasty little bitch that lives in your mind. Every time you want to move forward in life, to stretch yourself or to attempt something amazing and new she is there with her stink attitude telling you why you can't do it.

Do not pay attention to her, do not entertain her, do not give that bitch the time of day. Starve her ass out of your system because she was sent here on a mission from the dark side to totally fuck you up and hold you back. She thinks she's protecting you from failure and pain but oh no, she's keeping you small and from realising your fullest potential. Just when you think; 'Yeah that's an awesome idea I'm going to step into my greatness', here she comes with her negative attitude and backchat, with all the reasons why you can't do something or why your idea won't work. And then what happens? You listen to her bullshit and don't take action.

Don't get me wrong, she sometimes manages to wrangle her way into my mind when I'm doing something challenging. This is an example of what 'Sandra' (yes, give the bitch a name, it makes it easier to deal with her and very satisfying to tell her to fuck off!) said to me when I was about to pitch my audio programmes to an online company a few years ago.

"Oh, so you really think you're going to get a deal with Audible and Apple iTunes. REALLY?! You?!! You're a nobody. Who is going to want to listen to what you've got to say. No one will care about what you think. In fact, I wouldn't even waste your time pitching the idea, I'd just give up now and save yourself the embarrassment."

So, as you can see, it ain't much fun having a Sandra lurking around. The best thing you can do is turn that bitch into a beast who's going to make you ROAR!!

#makemeroar

Here are some examples of limiting beliefs that could have been cultivated in childhood which are no longer useful as an adult:

I'm rubbish at... playing musical instruments, learning languages, sports, maths.

Rich people are... lucky, greedy, horrible, born with a silver spoon in their mouths.

Money... doesn't grow on trees, you have to work hard for money, it is the devil.

A job... is just to pay the bills, something you get only if you go to university, it is not fun.

Now you're an adult it's great if you can identify your limiting beliefs and pull the rug from underneath them so that you can learn how to condition your own mind.

What are you rubbish at? *(e.g., maths, meeting men, managing money)*

Where did that belief originate? *(e.g., teachers at school, parents, older sibling)*

_____

_____

_____

_____

_____

_____

_____

_____

_____

_____

Do you feel that this viewpoint still serves you in a positive way?

_____

_____

_____

_____

_____

_____

_____

_____

_____

What would be a new more empowering viewpoint that you can really own? *(e.g., If I took a class I can easily brush up on my maths skills, or it doesn't fucking matter because I've got a calculator on my phone and I'm not afraid to use it.)*

"I'm not interested in your limiting beliefs, I'm interested in what makes you limitless."

Brendon Berchard

The main problem with these bullshit beliefs is that they often create a disconnect between what you *think* you want and what your beliefs have programmed you to want. For example, you may be thinking, 'I want to make shitloads of money'. But if growing up all your parents did was fight about money because there wasn't enough to go around, you will associate arguments, pain, and losing love with money. So, you may appear to go after that goal with gusto but deep down not really go full out because you don't want any hurt or pain. This in turn means because you didn't really try and you won't get that big stash of cash.

Another route this same underlying limiting belief could take is that you do actually work your ass off and make the amount of money you've always dreamed of, but then squander it all away so that you don't have it anymore. Because if you don't have it anymore you avoid the risk of having any possible future pain, arguments or losing love in your life. So essentially with this kind of limiting belief you will never be comfortable around money. Can you see how these beliefs can really mess you up?

The main reason we keep these beliefs hanging around is because they can make us feel quite cosy and keep us nicely in our comfort zone. They don't serve us but we'd rather hang onto them like a kid's comfort blanket for grownups. And the reason we hang onto beliefs is subconscious too, but if you do a little digging you'll soon stumble across why you're hanging onto yours. For instance, if you're overweight and you always say: "Oh I can't lose weight, I've tried every exercise plan under the sun and nothing works for me." The comforter here is that if nothing works then you don't need to try. So, instead of hitting the gym you remain nice and comfy on your sofa, munching on those delicious treats, and you don't lose any weight, which reinforces your belief that you can't lose weight. Or it could be that your friends are a similar size to you and subconsciously you are worried that they may judge you or not like you any more if you lose weight, so again you don't really give it 100%, which has the same result.

This is one of those times when you need to get real deep with yourself and not be afraid to dig down to reveal the truth. This is all for you, so open up petal and let's do this!

Let's see how we change this up, get rid of these shitty beliefs and get some new empowering ones.

Limiting Beliefs: Exercise
1. **Acknowledge the limiting belief (and tell it to get lost!).** *e.g., I can't run for shit.*
2. **What is comfortable about keeping this belief – and be honest with yourself, understand why you keep this belief hanging around.** *e.g., I don't have to get up early. I don't have to suffer in the wind and cold. I don't have to tell people how slow my pace is, which is embarrassing. I just can't be bothered.*
3. **What is it costing you by continuing with this belief?** This is where you need to clarify all of the magic that you are missing out on by carrying this

lame belief around with you. *e.g., It's costing me the chance to feel fit, healthy and vibrant. It's costing me the opportunity of achievement and feeling proud by completing a race. It's costing me the space each week to clear my mind. It's costing me a few extra pounds in weight which I'd love to lose. Fuck me, get my trainers now!*

4. **Write a new belief that's going to blow your bloody socks off** *e.g., With regular practice I have mastered my running. Every run I take I get stronger and faster, therefore I am a running goddess.*

5. **REPEAT** this new belief as an affirmation on a daily basis, hourly if you can, go hard-core to really set that new thought in your mind.

Now it's your turn. Think about an area of your life that you want to make a rapid change in now, *e.g., health, money, love, work etc,* and then think of the pesky belief that is holding you back and complete the exercise.

1. My Limiting belief is:

....

....

....

....

....

....

....

----

2. What is comfortable about keeping this belief?

----

3. What is it this belief costing me?

_____

_____

_____

_____

_____

_____

_____

_____

_____

_____

_____

_____

_____

4. My new belief that blows my mind is:

_____

_____

_____

_____

_____

....

....

....

....

....

....

....

....

5. Rinse and repeat

Think about your five most limiting beliefs and complete this exercise with them.

"Uncover your beliefs and pick a fight with them. They don't deserve to be in this part of town."

Think About Your Thoughts

Your beliefs affect your thought patterns and your thought patterns affect your behaviour.

So, it's pretty important to grab your tools and wire up your thoughts positively, which will also mean you're in tune with the Law of Attraction.

If you are thinking negatively you'll attract back negativity. If you're buzzing high on life, you'll attract great things. If you really want to get into the nuts and bolts of the energy field and how it works, Lynne McTaggart's book *The Field* is a must read – it's pretty deep, but well worth it. So be mindful of your thoughts and make them good ones.

The subconscious is a wonderful, obedient machine. It hates to disagree with you and always fights in your corner no matter how crazy you might be. So, if you tell yourself you can't do something your subconscious will find all the reasons and excuses to support that thought or belief. On the other hand, if you tell yourself, 'no matter what, I'm going to rock this idea until it becomes my reality', the subconscious will work just as hard to guide you to all the support you need to make that happen too. The subconscious mind also can't distinguish between imagination and reality, so whatever you feed your mind on a regular basis it will learn to accept and support. So, if you keep telling yourself that you are a loser your brain will not hesitate to find reasons to agree with you. Likewise, if you tell yourself you are an amazing abundant, happy, generous person your beautiful mind will also find all of the reasons to agree and give you a high five to that.

What are some of your common, recurring thoughts and opinions? What is your thought style? Are your thoughts on a positive or negative flow? If you're not sure ask a friend, not one who will tell you want you want to hear, a friend that will tell you the truth.

"Don't leave home without putting on your happy face."

If the majority of your thoughts are positive that's excellent, don't change a damn thing, keep that up, trust in the process and let the Law of Attraction work its magic. If you're more on the negative side of things and frequently turn into one of those nightmare whingy whiny girls, then seriously we need to talk. Put on your happy face. Remember the Pussycat Dolls sang 'careful what you wish for, cause you just might get it'? That is so true. If you're daydreaming, thinking, wishing and bitching about all this negative stuff that's what you'll get more of in your life because what you give it is what you get back. It's like a boomerang baby, and so your thoughts will affect your behaviours and therefore your outcomes. You with me? So, you think this guy won't like you, and you actually don't even make an effort to talk to him. Of course he won't fancy you because he doesn't even bloody know who you are. Likewise, if you think you're shit at a job, you'll approach it with lacklustre, so you most likely will be shit – and if you're shit at your job then it's no surprise if you get fired.

In the 1990s, a doctor called Masaru Emoto carried out a series of experiments with water entitled, 'The Power of Thoughts'. People must have thought he was a nut job because he was experimenting how thoughts, music and prayer affected the crystalline structure of water. He got participants to go up to a container of water and think really negative thoughts like, "I hate you, I wish you would die, and I'm guessing you're a shithead" – you know, stuff like that. Then others would go up to another container of water and effectively send the bottle a lot of lurve, with thoughts like, "I love you, you are beautiful, you are great", etc. And you know what, this crazy shit did actually make a difference to the water's structure. Say what? How insane is that?! The structure of the water from the negative thoughts was kind of angry and ugly and the structure of water from the positive energy was one of the most beautiful snowflake patterns you could ever hope to see – just breathtaking.

He then went further and tested the water without people, and instead typed out positive and negative statements on paper and taped it to the bottles, and guess what? Yup no shit Sherlock, the same result occurred. Ugly disjointed patterns in the negative water and beautiful symmetrical snowflake patterns in the positive water. And the scary thing is that in the average adult, over 60% of our bodies are made up of water, so just think about what your poor cells are experiencing when you are moaning your ass off like a bitch. It is changing the molecular structure of your body and not in a good way. If these thoughts can change your cells, they sure as hell can change your circumstances.

It's not only your cells that a shitty mental attitude will affect, but also your health – as cells make up your body, of course they're going to affect your health. Evidence now shows that headaches, anxiety and stress can be traced to negative thought patterns. And I believe that more serious diseases can be triggered in this way too. So be very mindful when it comes to your style of thinking and make sure it doesn't physically hurt you.

You've met those people haven't you? I can think of one client in particular. She continually obsesses about conversations she hasn't actually had yet, or what she thinks someone said about her, or what's wrong with her house when it's actually fine, and it literally drives her mad and makes her extremely unhappy, which then reflects on how she feels and then ultimately acts. It really wouldn't surprise me if she had a heart attack as she's so tense and stern all the time. Nothing in her outside world needs to change, just her own thinking. If she flipped the switch on her thinking, her life would be so much happier, positive and stress free.

"Guard your mind from negativity, like Supergirl from Kryptonite."

I can hear you say: "Ok, so smart arse, how can I stop these negative thoughts?" Good bloody question.

It's not hard, it's just something you need to continually practise until it becomes a habit, which can take up to 90 days if practised with conviction.

Rid your Negative Thought Patterns
1. Notice and acknowledge when you're having negative thoughts, *e.g., OMG I feel so fat I need to lose weight.*
2. Cut the thought pattern, just block it (like a crazy ex on your phone), with one sentence, *e.g., I've seen you now get lost!*
3. Remember you're a badass and replace it with a positive thought pattern, *e.g., go to the gym three times a week and feel healthy, happy and toned.* (And remember you actually have to go to the gym!)

Re-write the most powerful and positive replacement thought pattern for an area in your life that most concerns you.

1. Old thought:

....

....

....

....

....

....

....

....

2. What you'll say to shut it down, *e.g., not now, fuck off Sandra, you go to hell.*

3. Replacement kickass thought…

It can take up to 90 days to reprogram your mind and create this new powerful positive habit, which is totally doable for you, so stick with it and see how much better this thinking makes you feel.

Happy Habits

Positive beliefs and thoughts equal positive habits. Now you've got your super-empowering belief and you're kicking negative thoughts to the curb, the next step is to turn this into daily actions that will rock your world. So, if your belief has gone from 'I can't run for shit', to 'I'm a running Goddess', you need to align yourself with the actions and habits that a 'running Goddess' would take.

For instance, having the right running gear, joining a running club or having your own training schedule. The important thing to remember is that habits consist of continual actions. So, you will not be a running Goddess if you go for a run just one time. A running Goddess laces up those trainers and pounds the pavement repeatedly.

Have a think about your new empowering belief and what habits you need to support it.

What consistent habits and actions will support my empowering belief? It may be a number of things.

"We are what we repeatedly do. Excellence then is not an act, but a habit."

Aristotle

Accessory No 2 – Self-Love

**Putting yourself first in this busy
haze of life often feels impossible.
In order to flourish, take time to
reflect, nurture and love your true
self.**

*"Love yourself first because that's who you'll be
spending the rest of your life with."*

Anon

I Love Me, Myself and I

Self-love is the foundation of your life, your happiness, your success, your relationships, your wealth, your everything, DO YOU HEAR ME?! Without self-love you can't dream a big dream let alone live it.

Self-love is the secret sauce that gives you the confidence to set a higher standard for yourself and once you've done that, oh baby, the world better watch out because you'll be coming full force.

"Do you know who is going to give you everything? ... You."

Diane von Furstenberg

Quite often without realising it we rely on external elements to roll up and dish out happiness to us, and this is not the way a secure mind operates. Happiness is only located in one place, and that's within you, and it's up to you to set up your personal sat nav to find it.

Many of the women I know struggle with the concept of 'putting themselves first'. It's so easy to put their job, partner, family, kids, house, pets and anything else with a heartbeat (and without) first. So, they end up putting their own needs way down at the bottom of the 'to do' list and inevitably these needs never get met.

You need to decide if you want to be emotionally abundant or emotionally bankrupt. Think of your well-being just like a bank account. Do you want an account that's lacking in deposits which means when you need to make a withdrawal it's impossible because it's empty? Or would you prefer to treat yourself like a healthy, abundant bank account at Coutts. Here you make regular deposits to your health and wellbeing, you're feeling amazing and high on life and your balance continues to grow and explode. With an abundant account, you have plenty of well-being, patience, security, happiness and fulfilment for yourself and there's more than enough to pass around to the ones you love.

If you love yourself first and make yourself a priority everything else in your lovely life will excel because you'll be firing on all cylinders and stepping out like a badass bitch into the world. The more you invest in yourself means the more you'll have to give to others, and the more you give, the more you will receive.

And to all the single ladies out there, if you do want to meet someone, your love for yourself has got to be on point. If you're looking for a partner to bring something to your table because it's lacking in you, it's not the greatest foundation for a successful relationship. This is why in my training course, 'Attracting Mr Right' the first thing we focus on is the relationship you have with yourself before we even begin to think about who you want to attract.

"It's not a sin to sign up to selfishness."

Back in the day I worked as an air stewardess and I would often do the safety demonstrations. You know, that thing that most people usually ignore. Don't come crying to me when we crash land and you can't get your lame ass out of the plane, so pay attention! When I first started working there was a part of the demonstration that I pondered over.

Ahem, in my poshest tannoy voice: "Ladies and Gentleman. Oxygen masks are located in the panel above your head. In the event of a loss of cabin pressure oxygen masks will be released. Place the mask over your mouth and nose like this (ta da) and pull the elastic strap to secure." And this was the bit that got me – "Please fit your own mask first before helping others." What, I don't get it? Surely if you've got a child or your grandma travelling with you, you'd fit their mask first and then fit your own? How wrong could I be. If you put your dependent's mask on first you might not have time to fit your own mask, which means you are both screwed. If you pass out while fitting your child's or grandma's mask, you won't be able to help them get the hell out of the aircraft, do first aid or whenever you need to do to keep them alive. So, the moral of the story is, just in case you didn't get it, is if you look after yourself first you are in the best possible position to look after those around you. Got it? Good!

Being tired, stressed out, overwhelmed, unfulfilled, ill and bored are not the states that are associated with you being the 'bestest', 'baddest', sexiest, fiercest version of yourself. So, if you are suffering from any of these symptoms, your approach to your work, health, relationships, and your problems are going to be lousy. These are the states where your patience wears thin and you can easily start snapping at those you love. You feel like shit and can go from zero to bitch in less than sixty seconds flat. This keeps you playing small and safe.

Treat You the Way You Want to be Treated

Learn to treat yourself how you would want someone else to treat you... and not to feel guilty about it!

This is a weird example, but roll with it. Imagine you're a new car (see I told you, and I haven't even had a glass of wine, yet!) and someone just bought you. How would you want your new owner to treat you? Would you want them wheel spinning off the drive and speeding around town at 100 miles an hour? Or, do you want them to drive nice and safely? Would you want them to keep you clean inside and out or be filled with trash and covered in dust? And how do they maintain you? Do you want an owner who tops up your oil, tyre pressure and takes you for a regular service or someone who doesn't care and only takes you to the mechanic once you've had a failure? I'm guessing you'd prefer to be owned by the safe, caring owner.

Thankfully you're not a car, but you are a person who deserves your body and mind to be treated like a queen. Love and respect your body and mind for a lifetime because no one is going to take better care of you than you.

"The history of all times, and of today especially, teaches that... women will be forgotten if they forget to think about themselves."

Facebook Poetry Page

Self-appreciation is something we don't often have the time or inclination to do. It's more common and a lot easier for us to be down on ourselves than to big ourselves up. But I believe this is an essential ingredient when it comes to taking the best care of yourself. It can have a bit of the ick factor and we can feel selfish for wanting to put ourselves first but that doesn't mean we're doing that at the detriment of others. It would in fact be for the benefit of others.

Bat-shit Crazy Celebrations

I love tooting my own horn and when I do something great I'll tell myself that I'm proud of me, and give myself a high five. I'll be running around like a crazy chick screaming: "Fuck yeah, I just aced that." So, if I beat a personal best at the gym, or another new amazing client wants to work with me I'll mentally acknowledge that I've done a great job, and tell myself well done and I feel oh so good when I do that. The feeling is like natural organic drugs that make you high on life, I love it! It is still fun to celebrate and be congratulated by those around you but it's extremely satisfying to know that within yourself, you know that your praise is enough. So, when you nail it, smash it, ace it, go bat-shit crazy for your own success. They should hear you down the street. You'll love that feeling so much you'll want to be doing things you can celebrate again and again.

A fun habit that I'm proud to have is that every single day I look in the mirror and say to myself: "I love you". I bet you tell other people you love them so why the hell not tell yourself? Fill up your own cup of love before you fill up the cup for others.

If you've got haters they might be bitching behind your back and say: "Oh look at her, she loves herself." Don't be angry, be ecstatic... whoop whoop!! If someone says that about me, I'm like: "Amen, yes I do love myself and thank you for noticing." It's not a crime. It's exactly the kind of vibe that should be exuding from every pore of your body. Ain't nothing wrong with love and what's the alternative? Walk around like you hate yourself, no thanks, I'll pass. That's no good for anyone.

"To be in love with yourself is the greatest love story of all."

When was the last time you took a long hard look at yourself and verbalised what you love about you? I'm guessing it's been a while, so let's not hang around, let's get cracking.

I want you to remember and really own exactly why you are an incredibly awesome woman? Don't go all shy on me or feel stupid. Really go full throttle on this. Let all that great energy out and get all that essence on paper.

You're going to write out: "I love myself because…" and fill in all those crazy cute qualities that make you, you. And don't just write the answer, be sure to write out the whole sentence "I love myself because…" each time.

Your pen should be like a tornado on this paper and writing so much that you're like: "I need me some more paper"!

I love myself because…

If you struggle with the exercise think about the great things that your friends, family, neighbours or colleagues would say about you if they were being asked about you in an interview. Really think about your beautiful qualities inside and out that make you the person you are today.

Repeat your favourite lines from this exercise as daily affirmations to condition your mind to listen, trust and believe what you are saying.

Who Are You?

To create fulfilment and self-love, it's important to be the type of person you want to see in the world.

Let's imagine the world was made up of seven billion people just like you, scary thought I know! Joking aside, what kind of a world would that be?

"Be the type of person you want to see in the world – a kind-hearted, forward moving Goddess!"

This has nothing to do with dollars in your bank or what job you do, it's about the important factors such as your character, personality, integrity and intent. If these seven billion people had your thoughts, your attitude and your behaviours, how would society be functioning? Are you the type of person that is going to help or hinder this planet? No one wants to admit that sometimes they can be a bitch but let's be honest. Do you nag, gossip or moan when you don't need to? Are you shying away from any of your responsibilities meaning someone else has to pick up the slack? Are you treating other people in way that reflects well on you?

"There's nothing uglier than a bad attitude."

There is too much hatred of so many different kinds in existence and often we ask ourselves what can we do?

If others are acting nasty or evil, (it could be people you know or those you see in the news) sprinkle your fairy dust anywhere and everywhere you go so you can leave a little more magic in the world. We sure as hell need it. You can be at the centre of creating a world with love, laughter, giving, great energy and naturally happy people.

So be honest with yourself. Is there a bit of attitude you can drop? Could you stop being a demanding diva? Can you stop being a bitch and a gossip and make it your mission to lift people up instead of putting them down? Let me hear ya: "Yes I Can!"

Random Acts of Awesome

One of the ways I love to sprinkle my fairy dust around is by doing what I call 'Random Acts of Awesome'. This basically means being on the lookout for opportunities where I can help or assist someone else and sprinkle that magic we've been talking about.

You might be thinking what kind of random acts can I do to help others? Don't worry. You don't have to pay someone's mortgage off or buy them a car, unless you're Oprah. Some of the smallest kind gestures can made a huge difference to someone's day.

First, the three golden rules of 'Random Acts of Awesome' are:

1. **They should be spontaneous**
   If an act is premeditated (I know, we're not talking about murder) your intentions might not be genuine. You may want to help because you want to ride in on your huge white stallion and save the day, which means it's more about your ego than helping someone out. So, feel free to go and save the day but don't count that as one of your RAAs if your ego is involved.

2. **Don't expect anything back**
   When you are truly in a state of giving, you do
   not expect anything back in return. An RAA is
   not a 'I'll scratch your back and you scratch mine'
   kind of deal. It's about you giving wholly without
   expectation of receiving anything back in return,
   including praise, which you may well get but you're
   not doing it for the praise, otherwise you're feeding
   that greedy ego again. This is about pure, high
   energy being sent out to others.

3. **Pay it forward**
   If you get the opportunity or someone you help is
   in a position to do so you can ask them to 'pay it
   forward'. So, if they feel like you've done a good
   deed for them at some point in the future if the
   opportunity arises, they can do a good deed for
   someone else. It's not conditional but helps to
   spread these good vibes around the world.

*"Be the kind of person who sprinkles your magic
wherever you go."*

One of my recent RAAs was feeding a homeless guy at a train
station. He wasn't looking too happy when I passed by and
as I had time before my train, and change in my purse, the
opportunity to add a little sunshine to a stranger's day was
there. I popped into Starbucks and for the cost of a cup of
coffee and a ham and cheese croissant I changed a man's state
instantly. A man I don't know, a man I'll never see again, a
man who was less fortunate than me. I will never forget the
way his face lit up and how his smile beamed. The gratitude
was so heart-felt, it was as if I'd given him the winning
numbers to the lottery. It was so touching I teared up as I
turned away with the reminder of how lucky most of us are.

It doesn't always have to be a stranger. RAAs can work for people you know too. One of the mums from school sent out a group text asking someone to watch her daughter as she had to work. I offered to help and felt relieved that it was one less worry off her plate.

Give what you can, when you can, because you can. Energy is universal, what you put out is what you're going to get back and it costs nothing to help someone out. And you just never know when you may be in a position where you need help. I grew up broke so I fiercely remember the good people and deeds that were done to help my family out in our times of need, and now I'm in a position to help I do so whenever I can, even if it's just giving my seat up to an elderly person on the train.

The next time you see someone struggling on the stairs with a pushchair give them a hand. When someone's £1 short at the cashier cover it because you are blessed and it's only one coin. When you know your girlfriend's been dumped, pop over with a bottle of wine to diss the bastard instead of sending a Whatsapp message.

"You can give out shit or love. Just know that whichever one you choose will bounce back to you like a boomerang."

Put the Esteem in Self

The real 'how' to loving yourself comes down to how you build and continue to develop your **self-esteem.** The *Cambridge Dictionary* defines self-esteem as 'confidence and belief in your own ability and value'.

I define self-esteem as; 'the state where you've built confidence, motivation and pride from showing *yourself* that you're a badass'. It's all an inside job. You can't buy this self-esteem stuff and you can't borrow it from someone else. It can only come from within you so you'd better learn how to create it in abundance because it will be the driving force of your future.

Compare two days – one where you are super productive and get lots of important things done, and another day where you've just lazed around and done sweet fuck all. Which day do you feel better about yourself? I can guarantee it's the day when you worked your ass off and got loads of things done? Why is that? Because you were making things happen, you were making progress and progress feels good. And that good feeling will turn to a great feeling and inspire you to move forward with your other tasks, ideas, jobs and dreams.

I know of certain spoilt brats who've financially been set up by their parents and rather than build upon their fortunate circumstances by creating commerce or doing something meaningful, worthwhile or fulfilling with the luxury of their time, they chose to literally bum around and do nothing. It might sound like fun at first! But imagine a life with no passion, no plan, no action, no goals and no hope and ultimately a low level of self-esteem. I wouldn't trade that for all the Louboutins in Paris.

We're too old to rely on our mummies and daddies, boyfriend or boss to tell us how great we are. We've got to handle this self-esteem business ourselves. Some of the people I work with feel like they're seriously lacking in self-esteem but from my perspective they do have it, they just don't recognise it.

One way to recognise your self-esteem is to record the things that make you feel proud.

"Self-esteem is the medicine for modern society."

You may find it difficult at first but this is a great practice to get into. Look hard, there is always something to be proud of within you if you delve deep enough.

What have you done **today** that makes you feel proud?

What did you do this **week** that made you feel proud?

What have you done in the last **month** that made you feel proud?

What have you done in the last **12 months** that made you feel proud?

See, you have got self-esteem in spades and now you can start to recognise how formidable you can be without someone else having to tell you.

So, you respect and love yourself, but how do you show yourself that you love yourself? Remember actions speak way louder than words – you can't fool you. Everyone is busy juggling work, study, hobbies and family but are you making the space and time to do the things you really love? The things that fill you up, the things that ignite your passion, the things that you yearn for in your soul? Prioritise space for these things in your life and you'll find that the rest of your 'stuff' can fall into the gaps that are left.

In any given week, I know my daughter needs to get to school, do her homework, have a bath etc, so I don't need to prioritise these things as they are the routine things that will naturally get done. Likewise, my work calls and meetings are in my diary and will happen because they are scheduled and, you know what? I get paid for that good stuff, so that's always going to be a priority. As a result, I take the time to consciously decide the things I want to have in my life, for me, that are most likely to slip through the net if I don't plan them. On a weekly basis, my non-negotiables are a personal training session, a full body massage, three hours of volunteering, and at this moment in time a few solid time slots for writing this book and designing the plans and interiors for my dream house. Everything else will have to fit in and around my musts. And you know what?

Everytime without fail it all slots perfectly into place. My clients fall into the times I have available, my daughter gets to school and I can still help her with her homework. The bills get paid, the laundry gets done, I still hang out with my gorgeous friends and life goes on. BUT, it goes on with me putting my needs first instead of last so I continue to live life in abundance which creates a perpetual cycle of more abundance. I'm telling, not asking you, that if you want to up your personal game and satisfaction levels you need to do the same.

Running yourself ragged and getting stressed and tired is not a badge of honour, it's a slap in the face that you're giving yourself. I'm a pretty cool mum if I do say so myself and I want to show my daughter that having a family and 'doing life' is fun, adventurous, challenging and rewarding and you only get to do that when you put yourself first.

"Treat yourself as if you're the most important person in the world, because you are."

So, make a list of the ways you can show yourself a good time and schedule in a realistic time when you can make these things happen. Treating or looking after yourself doesn't have to be expensive or overindulgent. You don't have to charter a yacht around the Med with a hot captain, or hire a man-servant. The small things count too. It could be as simple as buying yourself fresh flowers each week.

"You really feel the wealth when you start to love yourself."

Write down some of the ways you can show yourself a good time which are not dependent on anyone else.

Examples: Buy yourself fresh flowers, go to a yoga class, go to the hairdressers for a wash and blow dry, do a detox, buy a pair of shoes, book that trip away with friends, paint your nails, read your favourite book or magazine, call a friend you haven't spoken to in ages, start writing your novel, book a massage, go for a lovely lunch by yourself, go to an exercise class, invite your friends over for lunch, enjoy a classic movie, buy the fancy bottle of wine, go for a cycle ride, have a picnic in the park.

Now it's your turn, what experiences would you, really thank you for and when are you going to do them?

Self-Love Action .... When/Date ....

....

....

....

....

....

....

....

....

....

....

_____

_____

_____

_____

_____

_____

Now you've highlighted some cool stuff that you'd like to treat yourself to, work out when you can realistically achieve them within your schedule and budget and go ahead and start plotting dates for self-love in your diary right now. Don't make excuses, just fucking do it!

Now you're a pro at prioritising self-care, you'll find yourself recharged and ready to rock 'n' roll with other aspects of your life. You'll feel like you've got enough 'me time' so you are willing and able to give yourself abundantly to all those around you.

"Be your own cheerleader and go stamp your unique mark on the world."

Mirror, Mirror on the Wall

In order to truly love yourself you've got to love your characteristics, qualities and personality, but you also need to love your body, that amazing thing that keeps you alive. There is a perception portrayed in the media, movies, magazines and online that we should look a certain way. So sometimes it can be hard for us to fall in love with our bodies when we don't look like a catwalk model.

As women, we've been conditioned to look in the mirror and find fault. It's time to tear that script up, get healthy with our attitudes towards ourselves and start to fucking love the reflection shining back at us.

This is an exercise I suggest you do at home when you're alone so if you're on the tube right now, you'll have to come to back to it later, unless you want to give your fellow commuters a thrill; lol!

Find a full-length mirror and strip absolutely butt naked, and I'd like you to strip that face too. So, if you've got any makeup on grab a face wipe or cleanser and get busy with it.

Take command of yourself. Stand up tall with a straight back and your shoulders down. Relax and take a deep breath. With love in your heart take a long hard look up and down your body. Then look into your eyes and really see you.

Look in that mirror and ask yourself what are the imperfections that make you, you? What have you always critiqued about your body that you can learn to love? And what is beautiful about what you see?

"It's OK to believe that you're beautiful."

Once you've owned these attributes and feelings I want you to write them down so you're reminding yourself that this is true.

What imperfections make you, you?

....

....

....

How can you embrace your imperfections?

_____

_____

_____

_____

_____

_____

_____

What is beautiful about the reflection in the mirror?

_____

_____

_____

_____

_____

_____

_____

_____

_____

_____

"You've said it, written it, now live like you mean it!"

Calm the Crazy

Another great way to look after yourself is to stay in the right mental zone, and I do this by being mindful. Being mindful or mindfulness can be or mean different things to different people.

We live in a time where everyone is so busy, busy, busy: "Yeah I'm just soooo busy darling." People are dashing to work, consumed by technology 24 hours a day, watching and hearing news that's mainly negative, trying to fit in family lives with exercise, time with friends, socialising, hobbies and studying; it often feels like there are – cliche alert – not enough hours in the day.

Life can feel nonstop, and mindfulness to me is about stepping off the wheel of life for at least five fucking minutes and gaining some space to find peace and clarity. It's a rare opportunity to just **BE** instead of **DO**. After all we are human 'beings' not human doings. When we take the time to step out of this crazy world into our peace we have this great opportunity to rest and relax our biggest tool and create a deeper connection to the universal energy around us.

Imagine being on the trading floor of the US stock exchange. There are hundreds of people all shouting and screaming; they're buying and selling and it's a pretty chaotic place. That is exactly what your mind is like. And you're trying to get a message about something you really want to think to this cool dude, aka the universe. But he's right at the back of the room and you have to claw, scream and kick your way through this raucous crowd to get to him. Imagine if you didn't have to do that. If you just had a nice clear room with no people in your way, just the big guy and you and you could just walk up, give him the message about your intention quickly and efficiently and then go about your day.

How much freaking easier would that be? Exactly! So, this is what being mindful is all about, it's about creating that space in the clear room so you can pass your message on to where it needs to go without the fuss and ongoing chatter of your conscious mind that never seems to want to shut the fuck up. It's also a place where you get to receive your greatest ideas, wisdom, clarification and guidance. Our minds are switched on 24/7 so it's great to allow some respite before they descend into overdrive and find peace.

To step off the crazy wheel of life and just 'be' means to be quiet, to be present in the moment and focused on your own thoughts. This can be achieved in various different ways so find a way that works for you.

Arianna Huffington, remarkable business woman, author and founder of the *Huffington Post* said in her book *Thrive*: "No longer is meditation seen as some sort of new age escape from the world. It's increasingly seen for what it is, a practice that helps us be in the world in a way that is more productive, more engaged, healthier and less stressful."

I find mindfulness through meditation and yoga. For meditation, I alternate between using a guided meditation app when I go to sleep, which is fantastic if you are just starting out, and just being still with my thoughts which is really hard at first but gets easier over time. The best thing to do when starting if you are just being still with your thoughts is to start out for say five minutes and build up slowly to longer periods of time.

Switch your phone to silent so you don't get any annoying emails or texts, and set an alarm so that you're not worrying about the time when you're in the zone. I meditate on the floor of my sun lounge and use the oven timer so that I don't have to keep my phone or any other technology near me. Then I just lay or sit down with a straight back and relaxed posture and close my eyes. I don't start chanting like a Buddhist monk. I like to take deep breaths into my stomach and chest, hold for a few seconds then release slowly; it makes me feel as light as a feather. While I'm doing this, I like to focus on a word or theme to stop my mind from drifting. Some of my favourites words to focus on are, gratefulness, patience, growth, love – obviously you can use a word that is relevant to you. Then just calm your mind and switch off your thoughts, which of course is hard to do, but like with anything you'll get better with practice.

I also love doing yoga as I find it gives me the same sense of calm and clarity and feels so good for my body. I go to a weekly yoga class with a great teacher and I also get up at 6 am to do yoga first thing in the morning, it's a brilliant way to start the day. And, if you can start your day with the right intention the rest of the day is much more likely to be amaze-balls.

If this lazing around stuff isn't for you, you can be mindful in other ways that are more in tune with your style. Many years ago, I was lucky to have lived on the seafront in Hove close to Brighton and I got addicted to watching the sea view. It changed constantly. I enjoyed the calm waters on clear pristine sunny days just as much as the roaring waves when it was dark and thundery outside. I could easily spend an hour or so just watching the mesmerising view and allowing my mind to roam; that was my version of meditation then.

You might like to chill out in your favourite chair in silence and be grateful, go for a walk with gorgeous natural scenery or have a hot bubble bath with candles and a glass of wine. Do whatever works best for you.

Three ways in which I can be mindful:

1. ....

2. ....

3. ....

When is there a convenient time in my day to complete one of my mindful activities?

....

....

....

....

....

....

....

....

....

....

....

....

....

....

Make this time a routine time to be mindful.

"Find a way to block the bullshit out so you can be in peace."

The Power of 'NO'

It is so freeing to learn the ability to say no to others that I really think they should teach it in schools. Saying no to others so you can say yes to yourself is an important tool you need to acquire to look after number one. Your gut will instantly tell you if you want to go to the party, or not, lend the money or help friends paint their house on your only day off, so listen to it. If you haven't got the heart to say no to someone's face on the spot, don't give an answer straightaway. Use the delay tactic and postpone your refusal to a later time with a simple, 'I'll have to let you know later', 'I need to check with X' or 'check my diary'. That gives you a bit of breathing space if you need it. To be honest I use this one all the time so I have a chance to step away from the person and really decide for myself what I want to do.

Once you have decided: "No, I don't want to go to your bullshit housewarming party because I've had a draining week and I'd rather stay in, on the sofa in my pyjamas with a large glass of Merlot and get my Netflix on," you can let them know. You don't have to be brutally honest, let's not hurt anyone's feelings, but at the same time you **DO NOT need to justify your decision making to other people**, you are a grown ass adult, with your own mind. Some people feel so bad saying no to others they feel the need to over-explain or exaggerate why they are saying no. Don't do that, it's totally unnecessary and you end up with crappy excuses that sound like: "I really want to come, I'd love to, but my neighbours have gone on holiday and I'm looking after their dog and I have to walk it every two hours and it needs to eat my homework and I've got to clean up their place because it trashed their house and they're back tomorrow." Fucking liar, people can probably smell the bullshit coming out of your mouth. If it's a no, just say NO. Let's do this the dignified and refined way. A simple: "No I can't make it but thank you for the invite," will suffice, and is much healthier than lying your ass off or worse still, doing the thing that you really don't want to while inwardly moaning like a bitch the whole time.

"A 'No' to others means a 'Yes' to yourself."

The more you learn to listen to your gut and say no, the easier and more natural it becomes. So I freaking dare you, the next time some schmuck asks you to help them again or attend some crappy event, or ask for a loan, stand in your truth, smile and just say 'no'. This is a wonderful gift to yourself to ensure you are not being taken advantage of and are focusing on doing the things that are truly important to you.

What is something you want to say a big fat NO to?

....

....

....

....

....

....

....

....

....

How can you say no in a constructive way?

How will you feel once you've said no?

What do you gain by saying 'no'?

....

....

....

....

....

....

....

Now you can say no to others you can also start saying no to yourself. You might think why the hell would I want to do that? I'm going to sound like my mother now but you'd do it for your own good. You might want to say no to using apps on your phone just before bed, you might want to say no to the lie-in you want so that you can be productive, or no to your negative self-talk. Whatever it is, use the same tactics above to point the finger at yourself and say 'no'.

I want to leave the cheekiness behind for a moment and get real serious with you. As well as being able to say no to the annoying stuff you don't want to do, it is imperative that you have the confidence to assert your 'no' if you need to when it comes to sexual, physical and emotional relationships. It really angers and concerns me that people are in situations where they are being taken advantage of and I want you to own the skills to say no when you need to because it might help to protect you.

If someone is trying to encourage you to have sex and your gut is screaming out loud: "This doesn't feel right," that's because it isn't so please just say: "Stop and No!" It's OK not to be ready. If you want to have sex and use a condom and he doesn't, say: "I respect my health so you have two choices, wrap it up or fuck off!"

If you're with a long term partner and he wants to pull a move that he's seen in a pornography video and that's not your thing say: "No, thanks babes, I'll pass!" This is your body, no one else owns it, you decide the rules, so don't be afraid to make the rules crystal fucking clear. Be sexually liberated enough to say yes to the things that you do want and no to the things that you don't. Likewise, if your partner is trying to stop you from seeing your friends or family and wants to control everything you do, and you feel this isn't right seek help from friends, family or someone in another safe place. And, if someone wants to raise a hand or fist to you, or hurt you physically in any other way, find a safe way to remove yourself from that environment.

Do not allow some asshole with no respect to treat you in any of these ways. How fucking dare they? Who the hell do they think they are? I'll tell you what they are, they're a c**t! There are more than seven billion people on this planet. Find the people that love you and care for you in ways that make you feel good. You know when it's wrong and you'll also know when it feels right.

"Raise the bar on how you want to be treated. If someone can't jump that high, they're out."

Gratitude Looks Great on You

Having a sense of gratitude is the foundation for all types of love. Cultivating this habit is not an option, it's a must.

So, how the hell do I do that Nicola? I hear you ask. We're friends now, so feel free to call me Nicci. First things first. It starts with an 'attitude of gratitude'. The very first thing I do once I've opened my eyes every morning is do what I call my 'gratefuls'. I spend a minimum of 10 to 20 minutes going through all of the things I am really grateful for like my gorgeous happy and healthy daughter, my own health and vitality, all the love in my life, having a safe warm luxurious home where I live safely, that I'm free to create my own work and have my own ideas. I'm grateful to have friends in my life who are beautiful from the inside out. I'm grateful that I have the opportunity to travel frequently. This is just a minute list of the things I am grateful for. I can usually spend 40 minutes doing this given the chance. I'm grateful about different things each day as there is just so much to be damn grateful for. And most often I am grateful for my open positive mind set and the universe that keeps giving to me in such an abundant way.

"No one steps out of bed being a bitch if they've done their "gratefuls'. You step out of bed with a spring, smile and a bad girl swagger."

You are blessed in so many different ways so I'd love you to take the time and recognise that. Pause for a moment and write down what you are grateful for.

Five things I am grateful for:

1. ....

2. ....

3. ....

4. ....

5. ....

Find a convenient time in the day when you can do your 'gratefuls' and make this a daily habit. It might be first thing when you wake in the morning, when you're in the shower, on the commute to work, or maybe when you're making out with your partner!! I think it's best to do this exercise first thing in the morning as it sets a great intention for the day ahead.

You'll be so surprised how good it makes you feel and remember the more you're grateful, the more you'll have to be grateful for.

"Be thankful for what you have; you'll end up having more."

Oprah

Oh, and don't give me any of that 'I don't have anything to be grateful for' bullshit, because you've got no money or live in a cramped studio apartment. Of course you have tons of stuff to be grateful for. If you can eat something today be grateful, if you have a roof over your head keeping you warm and safe at night be grateful. If you don't think you have very much to be grateful for how about I drop kick you into a war-torn or famine-ravaged part of the world, where basic survival is the main task of the day. Where getting a scrap of bread or water is considered lucky. Seriously, if you compared your situation to that, how much would you have to be grateful for right now, huh?

What sentence can you use to instantly reframe a bad situation in your mind to recalibrate your levels of gratefulness?

For example, at least I've got a roof over my head, food to eat, and I'm not homeless. I have people that love me, I have my health.

74

_____

_____

_____

_____

_____

_____

_____

_____

_____

_____

_____

_____

_____

_____

_____

_____

_____

"Gratefulness is the foundation for living a good life."

Accessory No 3 – Goals

What do you want? Having a goal means knowing what you want and how to make it happen. Once you define it take massive action to achieve it.

"Life without goals is like champagne without bubbles. Disappointing and it leaves a sour taste in your mouth."

Baby Steps

In the coaching and business world there is endless talk about dreaming big. Go big or go home they say. It's always about climbing the mountain or soaring to new heights.

I believe that in order to achieve our goals we should forget about dreaming big and focus on taking baby steps. First you have to learn to walk and then you need to build those muscles before you can run. You can try and climb to the top of the mountain on day one but that will probably kill you. So pace yourself, because you're in this for the long haul. Climbing to the summit in seven days is just as admirable.

The truth is without spending any face to face time with you I don't know exactly what your limits are when it comes to getting motivated. You're going to have to work that out for yourself, it's no biggie. To achieve any substantial goal you need to push outside your comfort zone because that's where the magic happens.

The trick is to determine how far away your comfort zone should be. One person's comfort zone could be 10 steps away and another's could be 10 miles away. Owain Service and Rory Gallagher discuss this very theme in their book, *Think Small*. Using data from behavioural science research they suggest that, '...in order to reach big, you need to start by thinking small... it's about adopting a mindset that focuses on getting the small - often simple - details right, that will set you on the path to achieving big goals'.

To me there is a fine line between how sky high or lofty our ambitions should be. Too big and you can become overwhelmed and scared into non-action. Too small, and you'll achieve a goal easily and effortlessly without any real sense of achievement because you knew all along that you had it in the bag, which defeats the purpose of having an impactful goal.

So now is the time where you need to do some self-assessment and take the lead and define how far you can push your comfort zone. This is YOUR life. So, if you cheat this you're just cheating yourself. You can take the easy option and live like the masses who do a lot of talking with little or no action, or you can stop accepting your own bullshit and start living life like you fucking mean it.

You are a Goddess, you do know that don't you? And you have all the resources you need within you to succeed. But you've got to learn to push yourself to your maximum.

It's time to decide what dreaming BIG means to you. Not anyone else's idea, just yours.

"Nothing is impossible. The word itself says I'm possible."

Audrey Hepburn

Find your own level of buoyancy that will allow you to push yourself to your own personal peak in a way that encourages you to maintain progress. Once you've pushed yourself and actually achieved a satisfying goal, then you can up the ante and aim for something bigger, badder and bolder.

My hot personal trainer Mike loves pushing me to my limits. When I start moaning that I'm starting to feel the burn and don't know if I can take anymore that is the point when he cranks it up and makes me do 10 more because those are the 10 that count. It honestly feels impossible at the time, but somehow I do what I'm told and knock out 10 more for the bastard. And you know what? When I'm done, for the first three seconds I feel like I'm going to throw up, but after that I feel absolutely fucking amazing!

So the plan is this. You need to establish exactly where your comfort zone is and put an X on the outskirts of that bad boy.

You want the level of your comfort zone to keep you awake at night with excitement not crying in your mother's arms. It needs to make you leap out of bed in the morning to get your plans into action instead of pulling up the bedcovers. You want to eat it, breathe it, sleep it, but not choke on it, suffocate on it or die on it. I love that giddy feeling you get in your tummy when you challenge yourself to step up to your greatness. Yes, fear and feeling scared, nervous and nauseous is normal, you need those ingredients otherwise it would be too easy, and if it's too easy you're not going to create or achieve anything special.

I'm one of those girls that likes to weight train in the gym and 'lift'. It's one of my things. Many months ago, I started doing deadlifts. It sounds kind of easy but of course that depends on how much weight you load onto the bar. I said to Mike that I would absolutely love it if I could one day lift my body weight, which I'm going to be brave and reveal is 65 kilos, and you know what, I love how that 65 looks on me lol! #loveyourself! At the time, I could deadlift about 40 kilos so setting a goal to lift an extra 25 kilos was definitely on the outskirts of my comfort zone and seemed almost out of reach to me. But I loved training and ever so slowly week by week I started getting stronger.

In time, 40k became 45k, and 45k became 50k and with each increase I got more pumped and then finally I reached my dream of lifting 65k. It was a huge moment for me but the most exciting thing that happened was because I'd enjoyed the journey and stretched myself more than I could ever have previously imagined I wanted that feeling to continue. So, at the start of the year I set a new goal to deadlift 100 kilos... yeah baby! I very slowly and gradually increased my weights up from 65k. Some weeks I felt like I was superwoman and could lift a truck and other weeks I couldn't lift a weight that was previously easy. But I never gave up. If I'd had a bad session I'd just say to myself: 'Come back stronger next week'. Fast forward six months and I finally lifted my current personal best for a one rep max and I hauled 105 kilos off the floor... BOOM shake the room!! Did you hear me in the back there I said 105 kilos!! As you can guess it felt pretty incredible.

It's a simple example of the beauty of dreaming small and taking baby steps. If I had decided to lift 100 kilos from the get go it would have felt impossible for me. Instead I chunked it down to a goal that still stretched me but that wasn't too overwhelming and I went after it with tons of brass. It would have taken a lot longer to feel that I was making any progress if I'd started with a goal of 100 kilos. In that time, I could have gotten despondent and given up altogether which is the mistake I see a lot of people make, and I don't want that to be you.

What are you currently aiming for that you now realise is too far inside or too far outside your comfort zone?

How can you tweak this goal so that it is set at your comfort
zone?

Why is it necessary for you to complete this goal?

_____

_____

_____

_____

_____

_____

_____

_____

_____

_____

_____

_____

_____

There you go, that's what I'm talking about!

"At the point when you want to give up, realise that you are just getting started."

Gotta Get Goals

This is the topic that really turns me on and I hope it makes you horny too. Get ready - it's about to go down!

Some people say to me that goal setting sounds boring? WTF? If you're not excited you better recognise the influence goals will have on your life. Goals are how you design the life and lifestyle you want and then turn that hotness into reality.

If you're one of those girls who's waiting around for Prince Charming to ride in on his big white horse with his fat wallet ready and willing to give you everything you want, you need wake up from that deep sleep and remember this ain't a fairy tale. Unless your name is Snow White or Cinderella you'll have do the work to achieve the things you want. Now that's magical.

OK so I'm going to ask you to step into an aircraft with me because you know I love to fly. I preferably like first class because if I don't get my warmed nuts and chilled champagne before take-off I can get a little grouchy. But for now, we'll pass by the first class cabin – I'd love for you to join me in the flight deck. Please don't worry I won't take the controls, instead I want you to. Yes, you heard me right, hop into the left-hand seat please. Right Captain, are you ready? Great, I'll be your glamourous first officer. OK so we're on the ground at a standstill, not making any progress or going anywhere fast. We're at point A. This bird was designed and built to fly so let's put her in the sky and get airborne. But before we do anything there's a question you need to answer which will determine your next course of action. And there's absolutely no point in revving up the engines until this question has been answered. And your answer is the most important decision you will make in this cockpit and in your life. The question quite simply is, 'Where the hell do you want to go?'

In order to move in any direction from point A you need

to know where point B actually is. It's your final destination, somewhere you desperately want to be, the place you are meant to be. Somewhere that will knock your fucking socks off, somewhere you know you belong.

What if you don't want to pick somewhere to go? Good question, unfortunately not good news though. If you can't be focused or bothered for a few fleeting moments to decide where you want to go you'll end up circling aimlessly. Do you really want to do that for the next six months, 12 months or five years? If you don't decide where you want to go now your course will be determined by the winds and you'll be guided by wherever they choose to take you, which may not be somewhere you want to be. It sounds like a risky strategy to me. Don't leave the fate of this significant journey in the hands of the winds. So take charge, pilot your own path and guide it with intent.

"Are you going to let life happen? Or make life happen?"

Warning: Rant Alert

I see people around me putting more time and effort into planning things like their holiday or the purchase of their next car in impeccable, excruciating detail for months in advance. BUT, they don't plan or have any goals for the major stuff, like getting their relationship mojo back, getting healthy, finding a way to make money doing what they love, studying, or finding a way to contribute outside of themselves. Who gives a fuck about the car and the holiday when you hate your job and you don't have a plan for a way out? Get the car and book the holiday but put the effort, time and planning into your true fulfilment first. I go on holiday multiple times a year #jetsetter. I do get excited

85

about it, but I book swiftly and forget about it until I need to pack because I'm so juiced up on what's happening in my daily life. And that's also why, when it's time to come home I'm not crying into my strawberry daiquiri. Instead I'm excited because I've created a daily reality that I love and want to get back to. And that's what I want for you too. I don't want you to feel like you need to 'escape' life to relax, have fun and be happy. Make that level the basis of your day to day life and to do that, you gotta get goals.

#rantover

The great thing about making a plan is that you can literally pick anywhere you want to go. The world is your oyster. And if you're not 100% sure aim for something that feels right or is just good fun, you can always adjust your course along the way.

OK, have you decided where you want to be? That's just fabulous.

In a nutshell, a goal is simply consciously deciding something you'd like to achieve or do, making a plan for how you're gonna do it and then just bloody doing it.

Don't be careless with your life plan, because you know it's only this major-ass thing called your fucking life. When you get to December 31st, it's beautiful if you can look back over your year and be buzzing about all the awesome things you've achieved and can be proud of. If I ask you what you've achieved this year I don't want to hear some lame whisperings about; "Erm, well, I'm thinking about doing x, y and z..." I'll stop you right there, thinking is not doing. If you allow yourself to achieve nothing year after year, you'll end up in place far from where you want to be and wonder how you ended up there. The future is always going to be there so why not design it the way you want and arrive at your future destination in style by putting in the work and plans now.

"Plan your goals now so you arrive at your future destination in style."

I want you to be juiced up about the new things you've done, the experiences you've had, the places you've travelled to and the people you've met. I also want you to be juiced up about the opportunities you've had, and most importantly the person you've now become because of these experiences, which include the skills, knowledge and the learnings you've accumulated all because you set some incredible goals. That's not a bad return on an investment.

Every year around November time I start to map out next year's goals. I go through the exact same process I am about to show you. Do some goals take longer to achieve...? Of course. Is it easy to achieve all of them...? Fuck no! Ask me if it's worth it... 100% yes, every single time. It's the best feeling in the world when you do what you set out to do.

In the last 12 months alone, goal-setting is the reason I've managed to donate a couple of thousand to charity. I've also travelled to New York and San Francisco First Class. I've skydived from 12,000 feet and knocked seven minutes off my 1/2 marathon PB. I've smashed my gym goals, had a girls' party night in Vegas with my legendary BFF Pipa and got amazing corporate and personal coaching clients. And, oh yes, and the most important one to me? I wrote this freaking book for your sexy ass. That's just some of my hot goals, and there's plenty more where they came from.

You probably don't give a shit about my lame goals and that's fine, but these were the things that were important to me. If I hadn't consciously sat down and spent a few hours with a mimosa in hand writing my goals, you wouldn't be reading this book and I wouldn't have fulfilled even half of the things that have totally rocked my world this year. I'm saddened to think that was even a possibility.

Thank fuck I took the time to write and obsess about my goals. What really scares me are the astounding possibilities that you could be leaving on the table because you haven't gone through this valuable process.

If doing outstanding things for yourself doesn't propel you into action, what about the effect that achieving your goals can have on those around you. How might your energy, enthusiasm and success rub off on your friends and family? It might help them set goals they couldn't believe were possible, but because they saw you do it they were inspired. How about the message you can spread, the money you could earn? What contributions to friends, family and charities are being missed or delayed because you haven't stepped up to the plate yet? Go for it. Set the type of goals that make you feel alive and can help those around you – they deserve it too, right?!

I bet you want more for yourself so get laser focused and delve into how you can rearrange your life into a mosaic of your design.

"Smash your life up and arrange the pieces into a mosaic of your own design."

Goals Etiquette:
- **Know what you DO want.** Not what you don't want. My clients have a tendency to talk about what they don't want as opposed to what they do want. I don't want you to put your energy there, because what you focus on is what you get. So, decide what turns you on, and focus on that vision.
- **Put it on paper** – It's OK to have a copy of your goals on your phone, computer or tablet but the act of writing your goal down commits it firmly to your subconscious. Your goal list will be one of the

most important documents you own. So don't write your dreams on a scrappy piece of paper. Have more respect for your goals than that. Buy a nice journal and pen and show the universe that your goals are meaningful and important to you.

- **Draw your map** – The actionable steps that are needed to get you from where you are now to reaching your goal. Some goals may only need a few steps, others may need hundreds. Break your goal down into ordered manageable steps that will lead you down the easiest path to your goal.

- **Keep killing It** – Even when you hit bumps and encounter difficulties along the way, never give up, keep course correcting until you get there.

- **Open your eyes and enjoy the ride** – Of course you want to get to your desired outcome as soon as possible but enjoy the process of actually getting there. Celebrate what I call the 'mega milestones' along the way and really appreciate the journey.

There is a sexy science to how goals should be written. Follow this sequence to ensure you ace your goals every time.

The Sexy Science of Goals:

Your goals should **stretch** you, push you or develop you in some way and be a crazy amount of fun. So remember where your comfort zone is and set your goals accordingly. Review your goals and make sure they make you gulp.

Your goals can't be vague, they need to be **specific**. 'I want more...', 'I want to be happy' or 'I want to lose weight' are not measurable goals. Write precise explanations of what you want. So, better examples would be; I want to earn an extra £500 a month, my loving partner adores animals or I've lost 5 lbs. Easy peasy.

Your goals must be written in the **present tense**. So instead of saying; 'I want to sign up for that study course', which implies it's a future event you could say; 'I'm enjoying every second of the study course and achieving grades higher than I ever expected, I'm a fucking genius!' Instead of this goal being something that may or may not happen in your future, you're now cementing it in your mind.

Your goal needs to have **mega milestones**. Milestones are the measurable markers which guide you along the journey towards your goal. Without milestones, you may waste significant amounts of time roaming aimlessly without actually getting anywhere. When I'm writing, my mega milestones are every 10,000 words I type. What are the mega milestones you want to achieve on route to your dream goal? Be sure to celebrate when you reach them.

You need a **date**. Yes, a double date with Hollywood heartthrobs Liam and Chris Hemsworth would be nice but what I really mean here is you must date your goal. You need a date as a framework to work towards so you know what actions to complete by when. You don't need to be realistic about your goal, you can go from being homeless to having a multi-million pound home. But you do need to be realistic about the time it will take to get there so set your date wisely.

Add some flair and energy so that your goals are lively, make you smile and feel all warm and fuzzy inside. They should continue to inspire you and kick you in the ass on a daily basis.

The four commandments of goals:

1. Thou shalt be honest with yourself and set goals that stretch the fuck out of you.
2. Thou shalt not accept other people's judgements on your personal goals.
3. Thou shalt not compare your journey to another's.
4. Thou shalt celebrate landmarks and achievement of goals like a badass.

I met one of my BFFs, Claire, back in the day when we were on a training course for our new jobs as cabin crew. I loved her energy and craziness. I mean, who goes out partying on a Sunday night when you're in the second week of training at your new job? She then waltzes in two hours late because she's hungover, makes up some crap excuses to get out of trouble and then aces all the exams with top marks, beating everyone else in the group with hardly any revision. How could I not love this girl? I remember as part of our training we visited a Boeing 747 aircraft on the tarmac at Heathrow and Claire and I – as we were having a good look around – entered the vacant flight deck. As soon as we stepped into that teeny tiny space she looked around and took it all in. Then she slowly turned to me and said: "This is where I want to be!" I was like, say what? We've just started a training course to be cabin crew and now you're telling me you want to pilot this thing. I admit it was a bit of a shock. But with words as confident as night following day she said: "I'm going to be a pilot, this is where I belong." Fast forward five gruelling years and after mega milestones of securing her funding, passing the tough interview process, gaining a place with limited numbers on the flying course, and learning to actually pilot an aircraft she finally passed her first job interview. She then took to the controls of an Airbus A320 and was doing her final checks before getting ready to depart on her first flight as First Officer... BOOM!!

#goalgetter

The first step of doing anything incredible is knowing that you want to do it and then going after it like a dog on heat. Claire didn't let the fact that the industry is dominated by men stop her. She didn't let the fact that she didn't have the 156,000 Euros required for training stop her. (Ouch that would put most people off!) She cranked up her game by demanding more of herself than she ever had before and kicked down all the doors on her path until she succeeded. So if there's something in your heart that you feel compelled to do, or someplace you need to be, set your goal and make your move.

"There will often be doors blocking your path. If you can't find the key, kick the fucking door down and if that doesn't work bulldoze the walls on either side."

It's time to get to work so that you can create some momentous goals that will be life-changing for you. Make sure you allocate sufficient time and space and do this exercise privately. If you've never done an exercise like this before it could be the most important, significant, momentous piece of text you have ever written.

Use the questions under the headings to help you gain ideas for what you might want your goal to be.

Take a deep breath and really hold this thought in your mind: 'This is my time, my one life, this is my chance to design it. What do I want?'

Home:
How do you feel about your home environment? Is it the place you want to live in? If it isn't, what type of home is? Is the ultimate bachelorette pad, a cute cottage or a huge mansion? And, where is your ideal home located? In the bustling city, on the beachfront or perhaps in the countryside? Are you happy with the people that you currently live with? Would you prefer to live alone? Or do you want to move out of your parent's place and in with your partner? Is your home in harmony? If not, how could it be? Is it decorated in the way that you want? Does it give the space and ambience you want? Do you feel safe there? For your home goal, think about where you would live? In

what type of home and with whom? What kind of a home is it in terms of design and atmosphere?

My Home Goal:

_____

_____

_____

_____

_____

_____

_____

_____

_____

_____

_____

_____

Date I will achieve this home goal?

_____

Health & Fitness:

How do you feel about your general state of health and fitness? How do you feel when you wake up? Are you exhausted or excited? Do you need a coffee to jumpstart your day or is your natural energy enough? When was the last time you worked up a sweat by exercising? Do you feel light and fast on your feet or are you slow and sluggish? What would make you feel better? What exercise do you enjoy and how can you incorporate this into your life? How are you fuelling your body? With natural or processed foods? And how does it make you feel? How is your mental health? Do you have time to slow down, switch off and reset? Do you have people to talk to when things aren't going well? Do you know how to start a process to lift yourself up if you start feeling down?

What does an improved state of physical and mental health and fitness look like to you?

My physical and mental Health and Fitness Goal:

....

....

....

....

....

....

....

....

Date I will achieve my health and fitness goal:

....

Work:

Do you enjoy your work? When you wake up to go to work are you in despair or delight?

Are you doing your current work just to pay the bills or because it lights you up?

Are you doing something you are passionate about? Are you making a difference in the way you want? Is this the work you want to be remembered for? What would make you happy in the area of work?

My work goal:

_____

_____

_____

_____

_____

_____

_____

_____

_____

_____

_____

Date I will achieve this work goal:

_____

Money:
Do you feel like you have enough money in your life? Do you honestly know how much you need to live the life you want (it may be less than you think)? If you don't have enough money do you have a plan to earn more? Are you managing the money you do have well? Are you repelling money by always moaning and complaining about it or do you trust that when you need it, it will come to you?

My money goal is:

Date I will achieve this money goal:

Love:
One of my favourite comedians Chris Rock once said you are either married and bored or single and lonely which was funny but that definitely does not have to be the norm.

If you are in a relationship:
Are you happy in your relationship? Do you spend most of your time with your happy face or frowny face on in this relationship? Do you and your partner show and tell each other that you're in love? Do things feel stale or alive? What do you actively do to keep things exciting and fun? Are you still there because you really want to be or because you feel like you have to be? What do you think your partner honestly thinks of you and how you treat them? Are you still an awesome partner or do you spend most of your time nagging and moaning? What are you both bringing to the relationship table? How can you improve your relationship? Do you value and love yourself?

If you are single:
Are you enjoying the benefits of being single? What things do you want to do or achieve while you are single that may be more difficult if you were in a relationship, for instance a solo travel trip? Do you appreciate the freedoms you have of being single? Are you enjoying single life or would you prefer to be in relationship? If you want a relationship are you actively doing things to engage with new people? Do you know who and what you are looking for in relationship? Do you value and love yourself?

My relationship goal:

....

....

....

....

....

....

....

Date I will achieve this relationship goal:

....

Contribution:
What are you doing that is benefiting someone else on this planet? If nothing, what would you like to do? Do you feel like the world is better in any way because you are here? Do you know what your talents and gifts are and are you sharing them? What ideas do you want to spread? What would people in the community say about you? What legacy do you want to leave behind you? What would others miss about you if you were gone?

My contribution goal is:

....

....

....

....

....

....

....

....

....

....

Date I will achieve my contribution goal:

....

You will be amazed what can happen when you start to put these goals on paper. I've experienced so many incidences that have unexpectedly led me towards my goals it's almost been unbelievable. So just start already, have your plan and execute it in fine fashion.

Be both fluid and flexible in your approach. You might have an idea of exactly how you are going to reach a landmark but the universe may have other ideas. And sometimes it plays silly buggers by knocking you off track and making you think you've lost the game when in fact if only you knew you were just warming up. So your journey may follow a different route or take longer than expected but keep the faith in yourself and your guides to show you the way.

"Dare to take a ride with your fantasies and you'll be amazed where they steer you."

Hallelujah praise the Lord, you've done it. You've written out some brilliant goals, I'm so proud of you. Right! Go crazy, dance your ass off, celebrate!

I want you to imagine right now that you've achieved all of these beautiful goals. Some were tougher than others, some took longer to achieve than you'd planned but because you're an incredible woman you did it. How has achieving these goals changed and impacted your life? Answer by completing the following questions.

Why is life better because you've achieved these goals?

_____

_____

_____

_____

_____

_____

_____

_____

_____

_____

_____

_____

_____

_____

How do you feel now that you've achieved these goals?

Describe the woman you had to become to fulfil these goals?

How can you now help and serve others?

....

....

....

....

....

....

....

....

Wow, what a way to live!

I'd love you to blaze on over to *Nicola Findlay The Coaching Diva* Facebook page and share your hottest goal with me and the team and allow us to share them with fellow readers. Your goal might be just the motivation someone else needs to get started.

When you have doubts, remember that of course you can fucking do it because if you couldn't you'd never have had the idea about it in the first place. Listen and act on your ideas. They are planted within you for a reason so take them seriously because these ideas can and will change your life, and you just never know, they could change the world.

"Of course you can do it, because if you couldn't you would never have had the idea about it in the first place."

You've now got the tools tucked in your handbag which you can reuse over a lifetime to make the unseen, seen. Now it's all down to you. You can choose to be part of the 10% that do, or the 90% that don't. So, make your choice and make it a wise one. I'll be honest with you, I know that 90 per cent of the people that read this book will get a burst of motivation and enthusiasm when they read the pages but as soon as the book is closed and it hits the table they'll revert back to their old ways – their old ways of living in lack, their old ways of wishing they could have more, their old ways of believing that success is for someone else. Don't let those ways become your way; you know you're better than that. Become part of the elite 10%. The 10% who know what to do and will get their freak on until they get it.

#WTF aka What's the Focus?

I am a firm believer in the boring but commonly used phrase, 'What you focus on is what you get', because I've seen it to be so true in my life. Whether I've been looking for the perfect parking spot, a cute outfit, a new car or the right man. What you focus on is exactly what you get.

We have an amazing function in our brains called the RAS which stands for the Reticular Activating System and this tiny part of your brain has the power to completely influence your life. In any given second you'll have millions of 'bits' of information coming at you through your senses. The RAS acts like a sieve and filters this huge amount of information so you don't get brain overload and explode.

So, its job – and it's a pretty important one – is to only allow quality, relevant, important information into your conscious mind. It's like a really hefty bouncer on the door of the latest hotspot in town. If your name's not down you're not coming in! We just want the good, high-rolling important info that is going to be impactful and resourceful for the life we want to lead. So the RAS looks to see what you are interested in, what you're talking about, what and how you're thinking, what's consuming you, what your thoughts, idea's, dreams or nightmares are and when it finds any information relevant to those thoughts it allows those golden nuggets right on through the door. But don't forget it works both ways, if your thoughts and feelings are mainly negative your RAS will seek out negative pieces of information for you to focus on.

Just yesterday I was chatting to a friend in the car and talking about a personal development seminar I was thinking about attending. I wasn't too fussed about it, but had spent time contemplating whether to go or not, so it had been on my mind. Then boom, a free ticket via email turns up in my inbox the very next day. Coincidence, I think not.

Another example that you'll probably recognise is when you want a new car, and you suddenly start to see that make and model of car everywhere, and you're like, Oh there's another one again, and I can't wait until I get mine. There were always that number of cars on the road, you just hadn't noticed them before because it wasn't important enough to you at the time. But now that you're thinking and focusing on that particular car you see the damn thing everywhere. It might not be a car that you want, it could be finally finding that outfit or piece of furniture you've been searching for. Throughout my pregnancy I kept seeing pregnant women or women with young babies everywhere, and now that I'm not pregnant I don't notice as many pregnant women around. Again, the same proportion of pregnant women are always there, but when I was trying to get pregnant I was super focused on it so my mind was tuned in to anything pregnancy related. This focus can be sent towards anything you love and want.

"Starve your distractions and feed your focus."

Anon

The pattern that I notice in a selection of my clients, friends and family is that if the focus is negative and you allow yourself to wallow in the shit you are only going to attract more shit. I know of people who are millionaires on paper, have their health and a beautiful family but choose to always focus on what's wrong with life. They feel they don't have enough money and never treat themselves to anything of quality or value. They feel they've been hard done by when they haven't, they frequently feel stressed and tense and only talk negatively about others. What spoilt, ungrateful bastards. It's almost like a badge of honour they wear and because they continually look at life through that dark lens, their negativity is always returned back to them.

If you find yourself wallowing in the shit, change your focus and remember what you have to be grateful for. Keep your focus positive so that your RAS can start filtering all the things that are going to help you out.

Where has my focus been?

....

....

....

....

....

....

Where will my new focus be?

....

....

....

....

....

....

....

....

....

....

....

....

....

....

_____

_____

_____

_____

_____

_____

_____

Awesome Things that I am grateful for in life:

1. _____

2. _____

3. _____

4. _____

5. _____

6. _____

7. _____

8. _____

9. _____

10. _____

"Go to lost property and find your focus."

Become a Manifesting Magnet

Once you've got your RAS locked down in positive mode it's time to start giving it an additional helping hand.

I absolutely love this topic of affirmations and visualisations because it has brought me so many amazing experiences – from attracting my soulmate and moving into my dream home to attracting all the people I want in my life as I need them, as well as loads of other cool things that would take a whole other book to explain.

Many years ago, I read an amazing book on manifesting called *The Cosmic Ordering Service*. I highly recommend it and it's one of those tiny books that you can sit down and read in one sitting. The author, Barbel Mohr, describes how we should imagine that you have a huge catalogue which contains anything you could ever want or desire. You can flick through it, choose anything you want and place your order with the universe and the universe will deliver it to you.

But this isn't a real catalogue you can hold in your hands, no, no, no. It's one that is only available in your mind. You can choose literally anything you want, but the biggest hurdle is being open-minded enough to dream a big dream and dare to ask for it. Yes, I rolled my eyes and was sceptical too, until I tried it and it fucking worked!!

The first thing you need to do is decide what you want. Have a very clear vision of what that looks, feels and sounds like. Then, just like in a restaurant, place your order by stating it to the universe. I might say something quite simple like: "Universe please show and guide me to getting my book published. Thank you." The hardest part comes after your order has been placed. You have to willingly allow your order to be received and actioned. The waiting game is the part where doubts start to seep into your mind and you can undo all of your good work.

Do your cosmic order to the universe. Put out there the thing that you most want, and then as Elsa in *Frozen* would say: "Let it go." Don't keep asking where it is or when it's going to be delivered because if you keep asking where it is that implies you don't believe it's on its way. The key here is that you have to be emotionally detached from the outcome. Some people love the idea of the law of attraction because they think they can just place an order and then kick back and do sweet fuck all. That's not how it works. Once you've decided what you want, the most important factor is that you need to get off your ass and work to make it happen. Only then will you experience a helping hand from the universe in the form of momentum, but you only get momentum once you start to take action.

"True manifesting is allowing the universe to catch up with your dreams."

Gabrielle Bernstein

The biggest event I manifested in my life was a natural birth. The process of labour is something a lot women feel is outside of their control. I knew pregnancy and the birthing experience had the potential to be one of the most physically dangerous, painful and uncomfortable things I could go through in my life and I thought: "Hey, universe, this would be a great time to show up and help me out if you don't mind. Thank you very much." I had attracted great things into my life in the past but like most people I still occasionally doubted the system. After everything my mother had gone through in her failed pregnancies it was a huge deal to me at the time to ask for guidance for my pregnancy and labour, and fully trust that it would be there. So, I ended up viewing this process as a bit of an experiment, and in my heart I said: 'If you're really there show me, pretty please.' I felt bad, like I was issuing the universe with a test or ultimatum. Give me a natural birth or I won't believe in you anymore. But it wasn't like that. I just, like people do, had doubts for a moment, but I didn't let those doubts hang around for very long.

During my pregnancy I loved watching the TV series called *One Born Every Minute*, which documented the trials and tribulations of couples going through the birthing process. You wouldn't catch me giving birth on TV if the universe came down and slapped me in the face! But, I'm thankful for the brave couples that allowed us to share such a private moment and get a glimpse of what it was really like. I remember one of the midwives on the show saying that the body experiencing labour was similar to running a marathon. As I enjoy running, that analogy really resonated with me. Marathons are a hell of a long race and they need mental as well as physical strength to get to the finish line.

The universe won't run the marathon for you. You have to show up, train like a beast, then you'll get its guidance and support. And, just when you feel like you can't go any further, or you can't run any faster, the universe will give you the strength and support, that helping hand you need to get the job done, and that's exactly how it went down with my labour.

I didn't just sit on my ass and wait for the universe to deliver a natural birth to me. 'Yes, waiter I'll have a natural birth with a side of snap back please.'

You might have a natural labour 'by luck' but whatever your mission is don't leave it to Lady Luck. You've got to work towards it. You will need to be in a state of action for the universe to help you out, as it helps those that help themselves. Lazy motherfuckers need not apply.

So, I went into training for my labour and I went at it like a crazy chick. My three biggest focuses were my fitness, nutrition and the most important one, my mind.

Once I was past the safety zone of 12 weeks, I resumed jogging albeit at a more relaxed pace. I practised pregnancy yoga, saw a nutritionist, and during my pregnancy I had acupuncture, massages and saw a homeopathic specialist. You get it, I owned it! Then I got down to the essential ingredient that only I could do, and that was programming my mind. So every day, from 12 weeks to the day I gave birth, I did my morning gratefuls, affirmations and visualisations towards achieving the ideal birth.

Affirm and Confirm

To ramp up the engine towards getting the birth I wanted, when I went jogging, walking or driving I would do affirmations. My main affirmation which morphed into a daily mantra was; 'Thank you for my healthy baby girl and easy and effortless birth'. The affirmation wasn't crazy, fun or dramatic like my usual ones but it worked perfectly for me in this scenario. When you're designing your own affirmations ensure that you phrase them in the present tense. Notice that I didn't say 'I hope I have a natural birth'. This implies that the event hasn't happened yet and it sounds like I have doubts about whether or not this can really happen.

If you are going to trick your subconscious mind you have to do it good and proper. Remember, we are after unwavering, absolute, determined belief and anything starting with I hope, doesn't sound too certain. So, imagine that you have aced your incredible goal, it's done, you fucking nailed it and you're talking to yourself on the other side of this incredible achievement.

Make your affirmation jump up and bite you on the ass. It should be the kind of wording that makes you want to smile and jump through the ceiling. Spice it up a bit, just like your sex life, so that it's not boring and it's something you can't wait to do, lol!!

Here are some examples of weak vs strong affirmations:

I'd like to lose weight before my holiday.
vs
Because I train regularly and eat healthy nutritious food I am lean, toned and rock my new bikini like a Victoria Secrets model.

Result – you are so committed you hit the gym like a maniac and sculpt your body to gorgeousness

I'd love to meet a really nice guy.
vs
Thank you and praise the Lord for my superstar soulmate. Our mutual love and respect is 'off the chain'.

Result – instead of ignoring guys who don't tick every box you give them a chance and unexpectedly fall in love.

I wish I could earn more money.
vs
I'm insanely grateful for the financial wealth and abundance pouring into my life from noticing and taking advantage of awesome opportunities.

Result – you sign up for the course, look at overtime as a gift rather than chore, you do a business plan for that idea you've had for years.

"Give that sexy mind of yours a constructive, positive, present tense statement that means the goal has been achieved."

What keeps you awake at night with excitement? Or jumping out of bed in the morning like a lunatic? What consumes your thoughts? What makes you go weak at the knees, besides Ryan Gosling?

Your biggest goal, dream or desire?

....

....

....

....

....

....

....

....

....

....

....

....

....

....

....

....

What is your affirmation for this goal?

....

....

....

....

....

....

....

....

....

....

....

....

....

....

Now you have your 'finger lickin; good' affirmation you need to make it stick. I'm a great believer in the philosophy of 'write it down, make it happen'. So, as well as completing the last exercise, write your affirmation on a small piece of card and place it somewhere where you will read it daily. For instance, you could tape it to your bathroom mirror, pop it in your purse or tuck it under your pillow and read it when you wake up and before you go to bed. And whenever those creepy doubts start to close in use your affirmation to shut them out.

"Let your subconscious see it, hear it, feel it and love it. Then it will work with you to get it."

Get Your Visual Game On

For me visualisations are not a chore, they are a relaxing process I really enjoy. The process is simple. Imagine your preferred outcome before it has happened. Visualisations may sound like a load of bullshit, but when you visualise, your mind believes the imagery to be real, it thinks it's actually happening and while it's in this action it's prepping and priming your cells and body for the real event.

Many professional athletes, sports people and actors use visualisations as part of their preparations. They train their bodies but they realise that to have an edge they must also train their minds. Will Smith and Jim Carrey have spoken frequently about their use of visualisations and affirmations; you can see their comments on YouTube.

"I visualized where I wanted to be, what kind of player I wanted to become. I knew exactly where I wanted to go, and I focused on getting there."

Michael Jordan, Athlete

Visualisations are like those beautiful dreams that you don't want to wake up from. I set aside time when I wake up, just before I sleep, and any part of the day where I can lay or sit down (for instance if I'm on the train or if I'm having a massage), to visualise my biggest goals of the moment.

Find some convenient down time to really focus on what you want in your life right now and to visualise living it. When you visualise your goal, see it in colour with as much vivid detail as possible. Increase the intensity by including sounds, tastes, smells and what can you feel. To set the scene of your visualisation think about:

When is this?

Where are you?

Who are you with or are you alone?

What are you wearing? What are you doing?

What are you thinking?

What's happening in the background?

What is the weather like?

What kind of mood are you in?

How do you feel?

It should be like watching a movie about yourself at the cinema. Once you are watching yourself on the big screen as if you're the hottest Hollywood actress, actually step into the screen and into your character so that you are not watching yourself but watching the scene out of your own eyes. This enables the visualisation to become more real and vivid. You may only be able to do it for a short time at first but you can build up the time as you practise.

Repeat this as much as possible, when it's safe. Definitely not when you're driving or you may end up over a cliff, which I'm sure will not part of your visualisation.

I'm a HUGE Formula 1 fan and I remember reading about British racing driver Jenson Button describing how he visualises before a race. This isn't some crazy 'loony toon' shit. He uses this technique, as most of the drivers do, to enhance his performance. He said: "I run through the race and visualise a lap of the circuit. For me, visualising qualifying is very important..."

And while we're on the subject, if you've got any VIP pit lane passes for the Monaco Grand Prix, please hook me up, that's a huge one on my goal list.

Before my daughter was born, when I woke up, or I was in the shower, when I went to bed and any other time I could, I would visualise the birth I wanted. I wanted to give birth in the birthing pool so I just kept on picturing myself in the water, smiling and then breathing easily through the contractions and being overjoyed when my gorgeous baby girl was placed into my arms. Yes, I wanted a girl and I wasn't afraid to state it. I know the politically correct answer you're meant to give regarding the gender of your unborn baby is: "It doesn't matter what sex the baby is; as long as it's healthy." Not for me. I was thinking, "I want to have a baby girl, a healthy girl. If it's a boy we might have to send it back." Only joking, kind of.

I never tired of doing my affirmations and visualisations, in fact, I looked forward to carving out the moments in the day when I'd be able to do them and found them really relaxing. I can't quite explain it but my affirmations and visualisations became a part of me, it felt like they were ingrained in my soul and I absolutely loved doing them.

"Visualisations are the surest way to see the future in advance."

The last task I did every evening without fail was listening to a birthing hypnosis as I drifted off to sleep. I really wanted my subconscious conditioned and I knew that plugging that record on repeat for all those months would have a huge effect. My mind programming worked and I knew in my bones that I was going to have an easy and effortless birth. My mind knew it and my body knew it. I'll tell you who didn't know it, pretty much every woman I spoke to who'd had a child. The negativity was astounding. I received numerous amounts of raised eyebrows and bitchy comments when I said that I was going to have a natural birth. I got told stories like, "Oh it was so bad there was blood on the ceiling", "Once you get into labour you'll soon change your mind" and my favourite one with the curt tone was; "Just wait, you'll see!" When you are in the zone and in hot pursuit of your goal you have to retain your level of unshakable, unstoppable belief. Don't allow others to throw you off your trail-blazing course. Keep your belief strong and firm in your heart and use the doomsayers' words as leverage to push you further towards your goal. So, to those that rolled their eyes and said: "You'll see," I thought to myself, "YES, we damn well will see, bitches!!"

So the day finally arrived, I woke up with cramps at 2.30 am, with the biggest smile spread across my face as I realised: "This is it!" Long story short, within 20 minutes of arriving at the hospital my beautiful baby girl was born. Just thinking about it makes me want to cry as it was obviously one of the most terrific moments of my life. The labour lasted just five hours 20 minutes and I was able to breathe my way through the whole dilation at home. I didn't make it to the birthing pool I had visualised as my daughter arrived too quickly, 'goddamn it, Melia, I wanted to try that out'! The birthing process was way better than anything I had affirmed or visualised. Like so many things when you focus and own an outcome you often get a much better result than you could ever have imagined.

So, after this experience when I consciously put my faith into the universe, I trust and believe it is there for me without doubt and I'd love for you to learn to do the same because this will set you up for life.

Right now, I'm halfway through writing the pages of this book and I'm just focused on writing. I have absolutely no idea in hell how these words will eventually end up in your hands but I know and trust that someway, somehow they will, they just have to. Now I want to know what crazy dream you're going to manifest into your life?

Think back to the goal you used to design your affirmation. Use the same goal to create a visualisation.

What part of your goal will you visualise?
(e.g., If it was a race, would you visualise the start when the gun goes off, when you pass your family on part of the route or when you cross the finish line and get your medal?)

Describe what you will visualise in as much detail as possible. *(Where are you, what time of day is it, who are you with, what can you see, hear, smell, taste, feel? What temperature is it, what are you wearing, what mood or state are you in?)*

What will you say to those that doubt your success?

"To bring anything into life, imagine that it's already there."

Richard Bach

Accessory No 4 – Commitment

You will encounter many obstacles on the journey towards your goals.

Learning how to master them will be the key to your success.

"Just when the caterpillar thought the world was over, it became a butterfly..."

Proverb

What's Your Why Got to Do With It?

Once you've set a life-changing goal it's easy to get pumped up with excitement and start floating on cloud nine. All the possibilities and opportunities that are open to you and the sure sense of how freaking amazing life is going to be will drive you wild. But hang on, I want to pull you back down to earth for just one second, I won't keep you long. Here's the thing, you're buzzing right now, I get it. But at some point along the road you're going to face difficulties which could show up in a number of different ways. It might just be a red light, which is fine, you'll slow down and when it flips to green you'll be on your merry way again. Next time you could come across a speed bump, it will slow you down but hey it's a minor blip and then you'll move on. But looming in the distance is something you haven't spotted. It can't be anticipated or prepared for and it's going to hit you like a lightning bolt. It's a sinkhole the size of a fucking crater and you've just driven into it. You freefall to the bottom and then you're stuck. It's dark, it's deep and you can't see a way out. You're basically FUCKED!! And, in case you didn't catch it, I'm saying that at some point in time this kind of crap WILL happen to your dream.

It could be any shitty scenario like your boss screwed you over, someone stole your idea, you didn't get the promotion, your finances ran out, your business partner wants to call it quits, or you're running out of time. This stuff happens around us, every single day so you better be prepared for it.

Whatever it is, something destructive will turn up to give you a big ole kick in the ass and kick you off course. And this is where most people go: "Fuck this shit, I'm done, I give up." But you aren't most people, you're smart, you must be because you bought this book. You just need to, must do, have to, have your secret weapon hidden with you at all times. And this weapon I speak of, a short, sharp blade to slice you out of any situation...? No. Oh, is it a sexy secret agent waiting to swoop in and save the day...? No. Then what the hell is it? It... quite simply is... your WHY.

Without your why, your dreams will perish as soon as the going gets tough. You need to know the reason you are pursuing this dream. You need to understand on a deep level what it means for you to make this happen. And you can't get all drippy on me with reasons like, 'Well, I want to be rich', or 'I just want to be happy' or 'I want to work for myself'. That ain't gonna cut it honey.

Why the fuck *do* you want to be rich and have all that money? What are you going to do with it? What will the money give you? How will it make you feel?

What is happiness to you? What does it look like? What does it even mean to you?

Why do you want to work for yourself? Is it about what you are creating, or is it about who you're serving...?

Why, why, why – goddamn it – why?

When you're sinking in blood, sweat, tears and pain to achieve your goal your 'why' is the massive leverage that will catapult you back to the safety of dry land and allow you to forge ahead and stay on track.

Your 'why' is the reason that when your friends are hitting the bar for happy hour you hit the laptop. Your 'why' is the reason that everyone leaves the office and goes home to relax but you go to work at your night job. Your 'why' is the reason that when you put the kids to bed your work is just getting started. You might be tired, broke, stressed or angry but whatever you feel, you still soldier on, because of your 'why'.

My beautiful friend Denise started out with nothing and has now built a very successful beauty salon with wealthy and celebrity clientele clambering to get an appointment at her upmarket establishment. One day I asked what motivated her to go from doing nails on the cheap in people's homes to building this luxurious thriving business.

She explained: "I had my daughter Shai when I was 19 years old and I was a single mother. Back then I had nothing. I remember one day when Shai was about six months old I'd run out of nappies and I couldn't afford to buy anymore. I called my mum to ask for £5. She was struggling herself and wasn't able to help even though she wanted to. I got off the phone and literally dropped to my knees.

"I cried my eyes out and thought what the hell am I going to do. I had to make a makeshift nappy out of a hand towel for the baby and that was the defining moment that changed me. I was never going to allow myself to be in this position ever again!!

"From that day onwards I worked my arse off, not for me, but for my daughter because she didn't deserve that life. I bought a notebook and listed all of the things that I wanted for me and my baby girl and set goals for how I was going to make it all happen." Denise spent over 10 years slowly grinding and hustling to secure her future for her and her daughter.

WOW, anyone else need a tissue? When she told me this story I had to dry my eyes afterwards because it was so moving and emotional. What resonated with me was the power of her 'why'. Look at what it moved her to achieve? And she didn't stop striving once she could afford the nappies: her why continued to be a powerhouse of motivation. She doesn't need to worry about the nappies now, instead she has the luxuries of a multi-million-pound home with swimming pool and tennis court to boot, and her Range Rover is parked upfront on the drive. But her why is the reason that she's made it here.

If you currently have a surface level 'why' and you know it's not quite deep enough don't worry, it is there, you just need to find it. Grab a friend and ask them to ask you what your dream is. And when you explain it to them, ask them to keep asking you what your why is until you start to cry like a baby or have a deep emotional revelation.

Here's an example:

Friend: What's your dream?

You: I want to start an online business.

Friend: Why?

You: I hate my job and I'd like to earn more money.

Friend: Why?

You: Well, I'd like to enjoy a better standard of living.

Friend: Why?

You: I'd like to afford nicer things, have experiences and help my family out.

Friend: Why?

You: Because when I grew up we had nothing. My parents worked in jobs with long hours and rubbish pay, year after year making huge sacrifices for my brother and me, giving up on their hopes and dreams because they couldn't risk not having food on the table. My father died unexpectedly last year and now I want to create something of value so I can start to repay that debt and afford my mother some luxuries and experiences while she can still enjoy them. She'd love to travel and go to a nice restaurant once in awhile. I owe her and I owe me a chance to make that happen. BOOM!! That will do it for me.

When you hit the skids, keep your powerful why in your back pocket because when any of the multitude of reasons come knocking at your door to knock you out, you'll need to delve back into your why and that is the only possible way you can stand back up.

"When life knocks you down try to land on your back. Because if you can look up you can get up. Let your reason get you back up."

Les Brown

Your why is a bit like your sat nav. You might find that you drift off course but as long as you keep your why close by you'll be able to programme yourself back into your route and get revved up and going again.

Let's give some attention and loving to the whys in your life. Just imagine where your why could take you?

What is your biggest work/career goal?

What is your why for this goal?

What is your health and fitness goal?

_____

_____

_____

_____

_____

_____

_____

_____

_____

_____

What is your why for this goal?

_____

_____

_____

_____

_____

_____

What is your financial income goal?

What is your why for this goal?

_____

_____

_____

_____

_____

_____

_____

_____

_____

_____

_____

_____

_____

"Your why can push you further than you could ever imagine."

The Fear Factor

You've mastered your 'why' but there might still be something looming in the distance to stop you in your tracks.

There is a disease out there which has infected us all at some moment in time. Some people choose to live with the pain inflicted by this rampant disease. And when this disease goes untreated it spreads wildly becoming more potent and deadly.

They call this deadly disease... FEAR!! And when it attacks you it is relentless. It makes you want to give up on all of your quests for more happiness and success. It can stop you dead in your tracks even when you're in pursuit of the greater good.

You know you have this disease if you experience any of the following symptoms which sound like; 'I don't have time', 'I don't have the money', 'I don't know the right people', 'I'm too old', 'I'm too young', 'I don't have enough experience', blah blah blah, you get the idea. They're basically a load of bullshit excuses.

But wait, there is good news, thankfully there is an antidote and one that is absolutely free of charge and readily available for everyone to administer themselves, but yet it is rarely used. The antidote is what they call... ACTION!!

Some people say you should 'Feel the fear and do it anyway'. That's good, but personally I think you should, 'Feel the fear and then punch it in the face!' You need to stand up to fear and show it who's boss. If you're fearful of a task ahead that's a great example of you striving to achieve something that is going to stretch you to your zone of personal greatness. And honestly the best, simplest advice I have for you regarding fear is to 'JFDI'... Just Fucking Do It! Action debilitates your fear; the very art of action and moving forward will stop fear in its tracks.

"Feel the fear and then punch it in the face."

One of the things on my goal list was to raise money for charity and do something that scares me. So I thought great, I can kill two birds with one stone (sorry birds), and raise money for charity by doing... da, da, da, a tandem skydive. Now I don't know about you but I don't usually make a habit of flinging myself out of planes at 12,000 ft on a regular basis, and honestly it doesn't seem like a natural place to be – you know outside of an aircraft rather than inside one!

So I was a skydive virgin and naturally I got a bit nervous, scared and was generally pooping my pants. The night before the jump my nerves were a mess and I was seriously doubting if I could actually do it.

I started praying, which is not something I do, I don't even know who I was praying to, anyone up there who'd listen I guess. All sorts of crazy thoughts started running through my mind, like what if the parachute doesn't open? What if the instructor I jump with has a heart attack? And, for some strange reason my biggest fear was that the strap connecting me to the instructor would not be fastened properly and I'd end up in free fall and plummet to my untimely death. I was even imagining the headlines in the local news; 'A young woman tragically died today on her first skydive in aid of charity...' My neurosis was so bad that I even thought, 'Well at least if I die there would be an avalanche of donations to my fundraising page so at least that would be wonderful for the charity and something good would come out of my death'. I seriously had those thoughts; crazy right? Can you see how bad I let the fear spiral out of control?

So yeah, definitely it's fair to say I was totally freaking out but logically I knew that the fear of doing the jump was:

1. Irrational. Statistically I was more likely to die driving my car to the airfield than during my skydive. Trust me I googled it.

2. The fear was worse than doing the actual jump itself.

And, I'm certain that applies to your fears too. Your mind is able to conjure up completely ridiculous scenarios that are most likely never going to happen in a million fucking years. These fears build up in your mind, get magnified and twisted into something that doesn't even remotely resemble reality and can stop you before you even get started. Don't let it. The fact I was doing the jump for charity was a huge motivator for me as people had already donated their money and I was therefore being held accountable or, as I felt, 'being held to ransom'. So I felt that I couldn't back out even if I wanted to. You need to find the reason why you need to shut up and do your thang; what or who will hold you accountable?

Once you commit to your task and start putting the wheels in motion you will find that your fear will naturally evaporate. Once I arrived at the jump site that was my point of commitment. That was the moment where I was like, 'OK, there's no turning back now, I'm punching fear in the face and I'm doing this', and voila the fear was gone. And the fear was replaced with a supersize dose of adrenaline which felt incredible. In the briefing room, I actually started getting quite excited.

Burn your bridges so there's no going back. Just keep on moving towards what you want, even if it's baby steps at first. Once your fear is in the rear-view mirror you'll be rewarded with accomplishments and progress that you never thought were possible.

Think about something you're fearful of. Who can hold you to account and will kick your ass if you don't do it? *(Family member, friend, neighbour, partner, boss, coach, me? Ensure that it's someone who won't let you slack off.)*

When your fear level is at: 'OMG I can't believe I'm doing this but I'm really excited too!' That is when you know you are in **exactly** the right place. Your stomach will be churning with excitement.

What form of action can you take to dissipate your fear?
(e.g., Agree a deadline with your colleague or boss... eek! Sign up for that event... eek! Book the flight... eek! Schedule that business meeting... eek! Post what you're going to do and when on social media... eek!)

Add action(s) and date for action(s)

_____

_____

_____

_____

_____

_____

_____

_____

_____

_____

_____

What will you gain as a result of punching fear in the face? (*e.g., Find out if someone is willing to pay for your side hustle, finish your work on schedule and get feedback, excitement and anticipation of an event and the urgency to plan training.*)

_____

_____

_____

_____

_____

_____

_____

_____

_____

_____

_____

_____

_____

Master Your Emojis

We talked earlier about positive thoughts, focusing in the right direction and shutting down limiting beliefs, but how do you maintain all of that on a day to day basis, especially when you might be having a really crappy day? It's hard to feel all grateful and blessed when you've just missed the train on the way to an interview or you've been on your fourth car crash date in row, and you're wondering where all the good men have gone. But it's something that you can condition yourself to do. People that know me always see me happy and carefree and I've had people say: "You're happy all the time aren't you?" Of course not, I am human. Sometimes I have negative emotions and I feel sad, worried or nervous and believe me I can do angry like a pro. The difference is I don't live there. It's kind of like your annoying relatives, they might pop in for the afternoon but they're not allowed to stay permanently.

You are the one that controls how you feel about external circumstances. Don't allow external circumstances to decide and control how you feel. It's a bold shift that stops you from being sucked into victim mode and turns you into your own hero.

"Make the frequently used emojis in your thoughts the positive ones."

We've got emotions for a reason and it's healthy to express them. So cry if you're sad, shout if you're angry but don't live in that state for an extended period of time because it's not the state that's going to be most productive for you. If your partner cheats on you, instinctively you're going to feel angry, and you've got the right to be totally pissed. But anger can't change what's happened. Have the conversation you need to have with your partner and eventually move on, together or apart. Once you've chosen what path to take, your anger won't help you forget and it won't help you heal, so what's the point in having it around? You might feel that someone has done something to make you feel angry. In truth they have made a decision on their path and you have chosen anger. If you kick the cheater to the curb you might instead want to choose a state, emotion or theme that's more useful to you like freedom or relief, because now you're not with someone who doesn't respect you anymore. If you decide to make it work you might choose, growth or forgiveness.

Consciously choosing your emotions and learning to reframe things and look at them from a better perspective will save you from losing your mind and make living an incredible life much more possible.

Shit is always going to be thrown at your fan, that's called LIFE, get used to it. What's important is how you clean it up. If you leave it and it festers, it's going to stink and you'll be living in squalor. Or you can clean it up. You'll have the memory that it was there but you can start living in peace again.

I've spent the past 11 years battling with a skin condition called atopic eczema. Some days it's great, some days it's truly awful. On the worst days my skin sheds drastically, it feels itchy, dry, sore and tight. It weeps and scabs over and the dryness spreads to my scalp. I'm pretty much house bound, save for an outing to get some strong prescription steroids from the Doc.

When it's this bad I feel stiff, sore and gross and mentally I'm beat. This condition was the reason I had to give up the flying career I loved because travelling frequently was causing me to dry out even more. At its peak I remember thinking if I had to live every day like this I wouldn't bother. Fortunately, I had good people around me to help and support me and I got through the worst of it. I wasn't actually going to write about my skin because it's not exactly pleasant reading, but guess what I'm currently in the midst of a nasty flare up and I thought hey I'm going to share it with you. It's been over two years since my skin has been this bad but the most important thing I'm doing right now is to focus on the solution and not the problem. I've had to cancel a corporate training day I was due to deliver but, hey they'll survive without me. I've had to cancel on a few meetups with friends but they understand so it's OK. What I did do was make a date with a Doctor and I've got the tablets and creams that I need which are going to make me better. And I'm doing my best to breathe and relax. So as I'm laying in bed ill, I'm putting my mind firmly on focus to all the exciting stuff I'm working on and the great opportunities that are coming my way. I've got my emotions in check and I'm not going to let this bullshit take me down.

So, we've all got our own bag of nails that we're heaving around, whether it's a health, financial, relationship or other issue. Sometimes others can see our burdens and sometimes

140

they can't. Just be mindful that at any given time, the people around you could be going through their own struggle and as we can't see what's going on behind closed doors, let's just practise empathy and love.

When the shit does come flying at your fan and trust me there is much of it to come, are you going to wallow in misery and allow your life to crash and burn or are you going to step up and do something about it?

So, stop nagging, stop bitching, stop moaning about every little fucking thing in the world that upsets you, especially the crap that really doesn't matter. I'm sure the people who have to listen to it would appreciate a rest from the bullshit talk. Instead put that same energy into letting good, great, positive, supportive words and solutions come spewing out of your mouth and you'll see how it changes your attitude for the better and how wonderful it makes you feel.

So, the choice is yours, when the shit hits the fan you can choose one of these emotional states:

A) Be a miserable bitch and hang this event around your neck like the latest statement necklace. Allowing it to weigh you down in thoughts and emotions which as you know is going to affect how you feel and act so you feel like shit, act like shit and generally life is, you guessed it smart ass... SHIT! It is basically a self-perpetuating downward spiral, which I would avoid at all costs like your ex's new girlfriend. And it'll give you a chronic case of the 'poor me' syndrome.

B) Learn to grieve, live with any sadness and pain but heal at the same time. Shed your tears for said event, feel sad, angry, upset, scared but then move onwards and upwards. You don't allow the situation to overrun or ruin your life. Learn from the experience, understand what positives you can take away and what direction you want your future to take. You are not going to be defined by this event, you are going to own it, deal with it and move on from it, baby.

"Stop with the pity party, and start a positive party."

I've had plenty of times where I've been in a position where I could lose it but instead I purposefully engaged my thoughts and emotions. Last year I was flying back from a trip to Rome and you'll feel with me on this one... my hold luggage decided not join me. Say what, yup all of my lovely holiday clothes, shoes and accessories disappeared somewhere between Rome and London Heathrow *cue tears and a loud rant*. Standing at the conveyor belt when it's empty and everyone single fucking person from your flight has got their luggage, except you, seriously sucks and that definitely had the potential to ruin my day. But I didn't let it. I could have gone into bat-shit crazy girl mode for sure but that would have done no good and wouldn't have helped my cause.

Instead I took a deep breath and strutted, not stormed, over to the customer service desk. With heartfelt, polite disappointment, I explained what had happened and asked when and how I was going to get my case back. The lovely guy at the desk didn't make my bag disappear so there was no need to lose it with him, and also this was going to be the guy that could help me get my bag back so why the hell would I want to piss him off by acting out? I was gutted but I reminded myself that everything in the case were just 'things', Jimmy Choo's and a Victoria Beckham dress can be replaced, right? And in the grand scheme of things going on in the world losing my suitcase was not a big deal. Insurance could be claimed on if necessary and it wasn't like it I was injured or in an accident. I chose to pick an optimistic emoji and save myself additional stress by going with option B. I went home and reflected on what a wonderful trip I'd had over a much-needed glass of wine. My luggage was eventually returned within 48 hrs, so you see, there was no need for me to let it ruin a sacred day of my life.

A few weeks ago I was watching the Formula 4 series of motor sport on TV. A young boy of 17 called Billy Monger was racing his car that day. He's a young budding talent who is destined for great things. But that race day at Donington will be one that Billy will never forget. During the race, he turned the corner of a bend and smashed at speed into a stationary broken down race car on the track. The crash was so severe it took emergency crews over 90 minutes to remove him from his car. The crash cost Billy dearly as within a matter of days both his legs were amputated. This is the kind of event that you can only imagine in your worst nightmares yet Billy's outlook and mentality has been remarkable.

Within five months he was back behind the wheel of an adapted car in a bid to regain his race license. I have no doubt that Billy will go on to achieve extraordinary things in his lifetime as his mind is focused in exactly the right direction. If Billy can look to the positive in the future when he's been dealt such a devastating blow, so can you.

If you've suffered a deep trauma of any kind. Coaching won't necessarily work for you because it's forward focused and you'll most likely need to look back to the past and deal with what happened. If that's the case, I hope you find the strength and professional support and help that you need.

Don't leave your state in the hands of the weather, a delayed train, an argument with your partner or a problem at work. Decide how you'll feel rather than be reactive. I live in England and I love it here, but if I cried every time it rained I'd flood my own house.

"I love the sun as it warms my bones and I love the rain as it cleanses my spirit."

Og Mandino

You decide your state from the get-go, so make it a good one such as gratefulness, optimism, joy or 'I'm awesome and I'm gonna smash it today'. When you are tempted to get angry or upset by life's annoying little tendencies, use a great tactic that I love, grab a pair of sunglasses. Not actually a real pair, an imaginary pair will do just fine. Put them on your gorgeous face and look at your situation through a new lens like gratefulness. There are so many different lenses you can choose that will enable you to realise that you are not in such a bad spot after all. When you put a new lens on your situation, things instantly appear and feel better.

So, with your sexy shades and new perspective the same event can have a completely different meaning and outcome for you.

Write down when you were last really annoyed about something. How did it make you feel?

....

....

....

....

....

What new lens could you put on this situation? i.e.
gratefulness, love, patience, optimism, growth?

....

....

....

....

....

....

....

....

....

....

....

....

What does the situation look like now? How does it make you feel?

_____

_____

_____

_____

_____

_____

_____

_____

_____

_____

_____

_____

That's much better, right?

"Feelings are like waves. You cannot stop them from coming but you can decide which ones to surf."

Anon

The major lesson here is it's really important HOW you deal with the crap in your life that counts. People will pass, you may fall ill, you'll have fall-outs with friends, you may lose your job, you might get dumped, but it's all about how you handle this stuff which is going to have you stray towards success or failure.

What was a shitty event or situation that's happened in your past?

How did it, or how does it continue to make you feel?

_____

_____

_____

_____

_____

_____

_____

_____

_____

_____

_____

_____

What will it matter in five years?

_____

_____

_____

_____

_____

_____

_____

_____

_____

_____

_____

_____

_____

_____

_____

_____

Time to pull yourself together: What are the lessons, positives, feedback, learnings you can take from this event?

_____

_____

_____

_____

_____

_____

How do these things help you with your future?

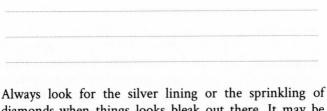

Always look for the silver lining or the sprinkling of diamonds when things looks bleak out there. It may be pitch black, but look deep and hard and find the lesson and hope that will pull you through and give you strength.

When things are bugging the hell out of you and crazy thoughts are swirling through your mind on repeat, one question that I get my clients to ask is: 'What will it matter in five years' or any other timeframe that works for you. Sometimes that shit won't matter in one week. So rather than torturing yourself and conjuring up all that bad energy around you, just ask yourself that question and calm the fuck down.

"When things look bleak always look for the silver lining or the sprinkling of diamonds."

Girl Squad

No one on this planet achieves any great feat by themselves. There's always some kind of support network to help on the quest to success, whether you want to be President, run a multinational business or climb the Himalayas. Now you've decided what you want in life, surrounding yourself with people who will support you is key to keeping your commitment.

Your life is your most important business and like any successful firm you can't run this ship alone. You might be the CEO of your life but you won't always have all the answers, so it's a wise choice to 'recruit' people around you who will essentially be your board of directors. They will enable and support you in living your ideal life.

This formidable crew which I like to call my 'squad' are an extension of your mind. You can't and don't have to know everything which means you can tap into their expertise and knowledge to fill in where you have gaps. These are the people who are there to help you push forward with your vision and your dream. Without them it wouldn't necessarily be possible or would most likely take you a lot longer to achieve your goals.

"Enlist your dream team to get your dream ticket."

The vacant positions on your board will depend on what your goals and aspirations are. Someone in their vivacious 20s who's looking to climb the corporate ladder and compete in an Ironman competition will need a completely different Dream Team than a mum of three who is launching her first business. The most important recruits to the 20-year-old may be a mentor at her workplace and personal trainer to get her fit for race day. The yummy mummy launching her business may need a nanny to cover some of her childcare and then a whole realm of people such as a website designer, photographer and copywriter. By being in tune with the universe you will easily and effortlessly attract the best people to you at exactly the right time. And what you need will always be evolving as you accomplish goals and move on to new ones, or take a different direction, or try something new.

Right now I have a small army of badass guys and girls on my Dream Team – some of whom I see frequently and some who are in my black book for when I need them. The important thing is knowing, understanding and implementing the right people in your life at the right time for what you need.

"He asked me my favourite position... I said CEO."

Anon

Every single person on my Dream Team helps me to create a lifestyle that I love, whether I want emotional, business or physical or logistical support. I implore you to find the people within your reach who will help you get closer to making your fantasy life a reality.

If you don't have the budget to hire the people you want around you, find another way to get someone's presence in your life. Read their book, get an app, watch the video's on YouTube, go to their seminar or workshop and/or do the online course. I'd love to do private yoga everyday but I find it time consuming to travel, so I find a great yoga teacher to come direct to me in my lounge through YouTube and boom, it's free.

So in order to get your business (aka your life) buzzing you need to decide what you want to do and who you need to make that happen?

What do I want to do?

....

....

....

....

_____

_____

_____

_____

_____

_____

_____

_____

_____

_____

Who do I need to help me make this happen?
Name .... How will they help me?

_____

_____

_____

_____

_____

_____

_____

....

....

....

....

As well as creating your Dream Team it's also just as important to note the people in your life that may need to be sent to the Sin Bin... indefinitely!!

For the people that don't serve you, or only bring negativity or drama around you, drop 'em like it's hot. You don't need that kind of influence in your life. Any form of a relationship is two-way and if you are giving and not receiving then it's time to reevaluate and move on. Stay away from the dream taker's the negative talkers and the bullshitters and build a tribe of people you love and respect and who love and respect you. You need people in your life that will lift you up not drag you down, so reflect on how you feel when you talk to people or spend time in their company. If you walk away floating on air, then keep that person around. If you leave feeling depressed and like: 'that was two hours of my life that I'm never going to get back' it may be time to cull the relationship.

I've had friends in my life that I thought would be around for the long haul. Sadly, they got fired because they were jealous, not supportive of my journey or just too much damn drama. It may sound harsh but who you surround yourself with will influence the potential of where you can go, so be very selective with the #squad you keep.

"Not everyone you lose is a loss."

Daniel Amos

Screw the Haters

A huge matter that can often bug us ladies out in a way that I don't see it effect the guys so much is the constant worrying about what other people think. I don't know why we do this to ourselves but it needs to stop! If you really want to strive and live full out, you need to stop giving a fuck what other people think of you!! Crazy ass fulfilled people do not give a shit what their neighbours, friends, work colleagues, family, school mums or ex-boyfriends think. They just get on and make their amazing shit happen. Go for that promotion even though you've only just joined the firm, start that business, write that book, build that house, study that course, do that race, buy that car, take that trip, enter that competition. Whatever is in your heart to do, just hurry up and do it already. Don't allow the fear of other people's thoughts and opinions to bite you in the ass and stop you from living in your true self. Be so in tune with yourself and your own truth that you don't hear the noise of other people's negative thoughts and judgements about you.

"Someone's else's opinion of you is none of your goddamn business."

Tony Robbins

Even if you hear through the grapevine that someone's been bitching, moaning or talking shit about you, laugh it off.
1. If they don't want to come and address you face to face they're not worth worrying about.
2. Someone else is spending their valuable time and energy discussing you. You must be pretty amazing otherwise why would they spend their time with you so vividly in their thoughts? If people are

discussing your business and stalking your Facebook and Instagram accounts and chatting about it without commenting or liking, then they're a fan.

I find it absolutely hilarious that people I know comment so much behind my back about how many holidays I go on, what I wear, where I go out, how I'm renovating my house, how much money I make... the list goes on. It makes me feel like a celebrity, people being all fascinated about my business. And it's so intriguing to me because I honestly don't spend time thinking about what they're doing in their lives because their lives don't interest me. I'm too busy focusing every day on how I'm going to make my life even more incredible and putting those plans into action. I just wish they would divert the focus back to themselves so that it could be enriching their own lives.

There will always be someone, somewhere, ready to add a running commentary on your life. The most productive thing you can do is NOT entertain other people's bullshit, unless it's encouraging and supportive.

"Don't worry about the bitches – that could be a good motto, because you come across people like that throughout your life."

Jennifer Lawrence

The truth is you do not know what someone else is thinking about, so until you do, don't second guess it and risk getting it wrong. You could have just wasted your time being pissed for no reason. You might be thinking: 'She was looking at me funny. How rude, I knew she hated me, I'm not speaking to her today'. And the truth is she could have been admiring your outfit and not had the confidence to ask where it was from, or she could have had a phone call with bad news that morning or an argument with her boyfriend. You do not know what is going on in someone else's life at any moment in time or what is on their mind.

If you obsess and allow other people's opinions to drive you to crazy town, it's going to hold you back and slow you down from what's most important in your world. So you just need to get over yourself and let that shit slide.

My dad is awesome, he's such a cool dude, funny, present and anyone in his company has a blast. Growing up I was a quintessential daddy's girl. He spent years in the army bossing people around as a sergeant. He even got shot during a tour in Ireland but took it in his 'cool' stride. Later on in life his path changed from hardcore military man to dedicated man of faith. Since finding God my father has only soared in my estimations, if that's even possible. I now find myself being the daughter of a minister of the Pentecostal church... eek! I very much value my father's opinion and will often seek out his advice, but on the subject of writing this book I've been somewhat secretive. I know my father will love the positive message and intention I'm spreading in the world but I'm not so sure he'll appreciate the style it's delivered in. So I'm kind of hoping I'm too old for an ass whopping. The truth is I want my dad to be proud of me but I'm on my own journey, and I'm doing it my way. So I'm not going to stop writing, change the title of this book, or write it in a way that doesn't reflect my own truth and he'll just have to be OK with that. If you start using other people's expectations of you to define your personal path, you'll end up disappointed and out of alignment.

"Stop giving a fuck about what other people think, so you can start giving a fuck about what's important to you."

Who is buggin' me out?

....

What do I think these losers are saying about me?

....

Is this fact or my imagination? (If fact, provide solid evidence not just hearsay. If imagination, then stop going cray-cray!)

....

Either way, why do I give a shit what this person thinks or says about me?

....

....

....

....

....

....

....

....

....

....

....

....

....

How can I start not giving a fuck about this and just focus on my life?

_____

_____

_____

_____

_____

_____

_____

_____

_____

_____

_____

_____

_____

"Fuck it, not to everything in life, but rather... Fuck it to everything unimportant in life..."

Mark Manson

Accessory No 5 – JFDI (Just Fucking Do It!)

It's easy to set goals. The hard part is gaining the motivation and confidence to follow them through.

"The way to get started is to quit talking and begin doing."

Walt Disney

Red Carpet Confidence

Confidence is an insanely beautiful thing because this power is the driving force towards creating massive change in your life.

Everyone can dream a dream, everyone can talk a good talk, but the difference between those who do and those who don't doesn't come down to being the smartest kid on the block. I mean Oprah, Richard Branson and J K Rowling never even went to University, right? And they did pretty well for themselves. More often than not it comes down to killer confidence and you're going to need this in spades. What I find fascinating is that people can have varying degrees of confidence depending on what situation they are in. Some people may feel super-confident at work. They'll be like: 'This is my zone, I got this! This is where I handle my business like a boss'. But in their domesticated lives it could be the complete opposite, so something as simple as hosting a dinner party for friends could be their worst nightmare and they fall apart. I'm totally not talking about myself *clears throat*.

It's a great idea to look at what makes you feel confident in certain areas compared to others? And a great question to ask yourself is how can you shift the qualities from the areas you do have confidence into the areas where you don't? For instance, using the last example, being organised in the kitchen and having all the ingredients ready in advance, having a recipe to follow, practising the dinner in advance as a test are aspects that you can take from your work life and apply in your personal life, to give you the confidence to cook that outstanding dinner and be crowned hostess with the 'mostest'.

Whether you are lacking confidence as a whole or just in specific areas of your life, know that confidence gives you the courage to chase the things you want most in life. Without it you could be kissing a lot of great stuff goodbye.

Do you really want to do that? It amazes me when you look at young children and they're so confident and determined. When babies are learning to walk they just go for it, they don't give a fuck, they're not unconfident. They see other people walking, and they're like: 'I'm going to do that walking thing, you know it looks kind of cool, and quite an efficient way of getting around' and when their limbs are developed enough they want to walk and ain't nobody going to stop them. Can you imagine if we had unconfident babies who were scared to even try walking? They'd be like: 'You know what mum and dad, this walking thing looks really tough. I just don't know if it's for me, because you know, I've been trying and trying and it's just not working out. I think I'll just stick to sofa surfing and you guys can push me around in the stroller for the rest of my life, I'm telling you this walking thing is just so stressful!!' Of course, that's a ludicrous and hilarious idea. These kids were born to walk so they just do it. They don't reach success on their first attempt, and it will be a gradual process like any huge goal, but do they think they'll be able to do it, of course they do. At this early stage in life they haven't been infiltrated by the 'negative police' so they just crack on and do it. They pull themselves up, they take a step, tumble back to the floor, but they just keep getting back up until they've reached the promised land, or in other words the other side of the room.

Throughout the toddler years, parents heap huge amounts of praise on their kids so that they grow in confidence. I think back to how I treated my daughter from the early years even up to now if I'm honest, and I realise that I always give her heaps of praise and sometimes for pretty lame stuff too. I just can't help it. I'll be like: "Yay well done sweetie you wiped your own bottom, well done!!", or "Oh wow poppet, you drew this for me, it's amazing (under my breath... 'What the fuck is it, no seriously what is it'). "Oh I see it's upside down," (under my breath... 'no still haven't got a clue what this is'), "Oh it's a bird (that looks more like a dolphin with a crown and a drug problem), but that's irrelevant darling your drawing skills are amazing. In fact, this picture is so good it's going up on the wall."

As adults, we don't all have parents who are willing or able to still heap praise on us like when we were a kid, so we need to find ways to praise ourselves and remember what badasses we really are. We have to be the ones to get ourselves motivated and find that confident, fearless woman within.

Over time as we mature, we start to doubt ourselves, and more depressingly we start to doubt others. Let's rewind and get back to the good times when your confidence bubble hadn't been burst yet, and confidence just oozed out of you allowing you to grab life by the balls. In order to do that I want you to complete the following exercise.

What have you achieved in your life that you are really proud of? It could be from any point in time so when you were a kid, at school or college to now. Include examples from any area of your life.

Examples:
Learnt to ride a bike, learnt to swim, passed your driving test.
Got your diploma, degree, masters, PhD.
Chosen to represent your school, college, university, firm, club in an event.
Cared for parents when they were ill.
Gave someone support when they were going through a difficult time.
Did a good piece of work at school or work.
Helped someone in need.
Got the job at, or started your side hustle, doing what you love.
Did x, y, z sporting event.
You get the idea, now it's your turn – step up to bat and add as many things as you can think of.

What have you achieved in your life that you are really proud of? For each answer also note your personal qualities, skills and characteristics that made these achievements possible.

Achievement – Qualities, Skills, Characteristics

You've just reminded yourself how truly awesome you are. Truly own it, and carry it around with you everywhere you go like the latest designer tote.

Now look back over the list of your qualities, skills and characteristics that you just identified and write how they help you build confidence where you lack it.

Area(s) where I lack confidence:

....

....

....

....

....

....

....

....

....

....

....

....

....

....

....

....

How I can use my qualities, skills and characteristics to build confidence in this area(s)?

"You are one fearless Feline – you just don't know it yet."

When I walk into a room, whether it's a boardroom or the hottest bar in town, I strut in like I own the damn place. My head is held high, I'm always wearing my sexiest smile with broad shoulders and I walk with a sparkle in my step.

This kind of swagger means I'm going to absolutely rock my meeting or have an awesome time with my friends. This is one of the things that confidence gives to me, what does it do for you?

If you are struggling with confidence, I've got three more tricks up my sleeve to help you out. But they aren't one-night wonders. They have to be practised over time until they become second nature to you.

First, STOP comparing yourself to other people. Remember the olden days when Facebook didn't exist? We were probably in a much happier place then. Too many people judge themselves based on other people's lives. You are on your own journey, walking your own path at your own pace. So, don't compare your route, journey or timings to someone else's. Be so concerned, mesmerised and passionate by what you are doing in your own life that you don't have the time or inclination to care about what other people are doing with theirs.

If you chose to play the game of comparison it is one that you will never win. There will always be someone smarter, richer, prettier, faster, skinner, stronger and generally more awesome than you, like that girl who can eat carbs before bed and still wake up skinny – what a bitch! Deal with it and learn to appreciate, love and develop the greatness that you have in YOU!

Second, set yourself a positive affirmation for the area that you are lacking in confidence. Because as you know, how you talk to yourself is going to affect how you feel, and how you feel is going to affect your level of confidence.

In what area are you least confident?

How does your lack of confidence make you feel?

_____

_____

_____

_____

_____

_____

_____

_____

_____

_____

Write a positive affirmation to dispel your unconfident feelings.
(Make it loud and proud.)

_____

_____

_____

_____

_____

_____

Say this affirmation with conviction. How does that make you feel?

That's more like it!

Third, and this one is like magic fairy dust to me I just love it. You can just 'Act As If'. This is the process where you step into the shoes of someone who could easily do the thing you are not so confident about doing. Someone who would eat this task for breakfast and spit it right out. Someone who you know would ace it. It could be someone you know, like a family member, someone at work, from your church, college, a friend. Or it could be someone famous like an actor or actress, singer, author (ahem, you could always use me, no pressure I'm just putting it out there!). Or my favourite one of all, the future confident you – your very own alter ego.

Beyonce is well known for naming her third studio album *I am Sasha Fierce* and for those of you who are not diehard fans you may wonder who the hell Sasha Fierce is? She is in fact none other than Beyonce's alter ego. It's who she steps into when she needs to deliver to her roaring crowd. It's who she becomes when she's filming her fabulous videos. She doesn't need to walk around every minute of the day in 'Sasha Fierce mode'. When she's relaxing with her family and friends and hanging out or doing exercise I'm sure she's more than happy to just be 'B'. But when she needs to step up a gear in life she calls on Sasha Fierce to help take her there.

Some of my favourite shoes to step into are those of 'Olivia Pope' from *Scandal*, played by the beautiful Kerry Washington. The character of Olivia was sassy, she'd take on anything and fight until the end and always tried to lead with her 'white hat' mentality of doing the right thing, a true gladiator.

Frank Underwood from *House of Cards* is another favourite fictional character of mine. Don't worry, I don't want to kill anyone I just love the fact that this guy just never gives up, like ever. And even when his back is up against the wall and he's in the tightest of spots he always finds a way to push through. You go Frank. And lastly, I love to step into the future, better, badder alter ego version of myself. So I will often say to myself: 'What would The Coaching Diva do?' and then I will automatically know what to do. When I was running my half marathon I got to mile eight and my legs said to me: 'You know what? I think we're done for today'. It hurt so bad and the next five miles felt like they might as well be 100 and the excuses and doubts started to creep in. So I said to myself: 'What would the Coaching Diva do?' and I heard her voice (well obviously as it's me, it's a bit weird) shout in my ear: 'Come on Nic, you're almost done, don't let all that training go to waste, keep it up, you've totally got this girl!' And what happens, I gain that inner strength and power to keep on pushing through.

When I have a disagreement with my partner and I just want to rip his fucking face off, I'll ask myself what the Coaching Diva would do? And her reply is: 'Even though he's a pain in the ass right now, you know deep down he's amazing and you love him. Be bigger, be better, and go and deal with it, with love', and that's what I'll do. I absolutely love stepping into a better version of myself because it's a reminder that underneath I really am that confident person, it was me all along and it can be you. Just gently coax her out and you will be astonished by the positive difference she can help you to create in your life.

Who are you going to call on to step into and borrow their confidence shoes? Choose more than one person if you wish. And you may choose different people for different situations.

You may want to be legendary domestic goddess Martha Stewart in the kitchen, American *Vogue*'s Anna Wintour at work and Samantha from *Sex and the City* in the bedroom.

Whose shoes will you step into? What aspects of their confidence will you use?

Think about the area you described earlier as lacking in confidence. How would your chosen person/people deal with this same situation? What would they say to themselves if they were scared, nervous or feeling hesitant? What inner conversation would they be having? When it's time for action, how are they standing? How do they walk into a room? What are they wearing? What gestures do they use? What do they say to people and how do they say it? How would they react? Allow it to give you the courage to get through what you need to do and keep using it until eventually that confidence morphs into you. Basically, when it comes to confidence, 'Fake it 'til you make it!'

"Own your idol's confidence like you bought it."

How would (insert name of your chosen one)

....

deal with the situation you are lacking in confidence with? They would:

....

....

....

....

....

....

Using what you admire about them, how will you now approach this situation differently?

"Whether you come from a council estate or a country estate, your success will be determined by your own confidence and fortitude."

Michelle Obama

The Spirit of Style

This is the fun part which I love. Some people say clothes maketh the woman, but I believe that truthfully it's your own radiance and confidence that really make an outfit pop. In Carmine Gallo's book *Talk Like Ted*, he says that confident people have the authority and that a confident look begins with what people wear and how they carry themselves.

In terms of body language, he highlights keeping a straight back, shoulders back and down, keeping your head held high, maintaining direct eye contact and speaking with good tone and volume as ways to assert your confidence. And if you do all of these things you will garner what he describes as 'command presence' and rock out like a true leader. So, once you have nailed how to master your body language it's time to move on to what to wear.

177

"Self-confidence is the best outfit. Wear it and rock it."

Anon

Don't dress to impress others but to impress your delightful self, and if anyone else enjoys the results that's just a bonus. Clothes can absolutely affect your confidence levels. I like to dress good because it makes me feel good.

When I have an important meeting, I make sure I look and feel the part and I enjoy dressing for it. It's so cliched, but when it comes to work and business, style it up and show up like you're the boss and *'Dress for the job you want, not the job you have'* because you know you'll be judged in the first 20 seconds of meeting someone new on how you've presented yourself – so put the fiercest version of yourself out there.

Former British *Vogue* Editor Alexandra Shulman said that: "Clothing is part of life in so many ways... As our uniform and armour for the day, as our way of defining our identity." So, invest in that power outfit for an interview or business meeting or those killer heels for a night out. And investing doesn't mean bankrupting yourself with shit you can't afford – that's what insecure foolish girls do. If you just bought a £2,000 handbag and now you can't afford dinner, you are crazy!

"Don't go broke trying to look rich."

Anon

Fortunately, as women, we are so lucky that we can buy clothes, shoes and amazing accessories from a variety of stores that still look great. I've got plenty of cute cheap outfits that teamed with nice accessories make me look like a million bucks. So stay in your financial lane when it comes to shopping, splurge on the cheaper stuff and save for your designer treats if you want them.

Also own your style full out. If you want to dye your hair purple, shave it on one side, wear black lipstick and pierce your tongue do it (as long as you're old enough!) and do it with pride.

Be comfortable in your clothes but more importantly be comfortable in your own skin, it's the only skin you have. Whatever your, style, attitude or swagger, don't conform to anyone else's vision of how they think you 'should' be. Go by your own brilliant definition. Sometimes I'm going out with friends and I know they'll be dressed in jeans and a t-shirt. That's great for them, because that's how they feel comfortable. But for me when it's Friday night, honey, I'm dressing up. The heels are coming out and cute dress is going on and I don't care if I'm out of place because that's how I feel comfortable.

"Real women don't hide who they are and they have no problem proving themselves to anyone. I know I'm real, I know I'm crazy and I flaunt that shit every chance I get."

Bitter Heartless Bitch Facebook Page

Even if you're not splashing out on clothes you can still feel on fire. A new shade of lipstick or styling your hair in a new way can have an amazing effect on how you feel. There is an enthusiasm and energy I get when I put effort into how I look and this isn't vanity. This is about pleasing yourself so that you can have the inclination to shine. When I take time and effort in my appearance and step out feeling amazing, that reflects how I work and how I play. It means I'm ready, I've got energy and brass and I'm coming for you, and I'm coming for life.

So, choose some outfits from your wardrobe or go shopping and buy some items that will give you killer confidence. It could be a suit, a pretty dress, those to-die-for heels or your skinny jeans that make your ass look hotter than the sun. Have a confident outfit ready to go with accessories pre-planned that make you feel like you can take over the world, and this will be your very own Wonder Woman outfit. Then go out in the world and shake what your Mama gave ya.

"Confidence is the sexiest thing a woman can wear."

Aimee Mullins

Sliding Doors

So, here we are, nearing the end of our time together, it's sad I know and I want you to take stock and realise that 'THIS IS FUCKING IT!' You ain't gonna get another shot at this thing called life so if there's something you're moved to do, right about NOW is the time to do it.

I want you to think about the stunning goals you set earlier and the difference, fun, adventure and growth that they will bring into your life. I bet that those abundant thoughts make you smile, right?

Although we both know that you could really start messing with life right now and make it win for you, there is a reason why you haven't done all of these amazing things already. Your fears, doubts, haters and lack of belief have all been jostling to get in your path, grab your ass and hold you back. What I've found to be hugely beneficial is to look at the pain it will cause if you let those bastards win in their efforts to restrain you.

"Give the middle finger to your haters, fears and doubts with a WIN."

I want you to think for a moment and look back at your past and think of the some of the things you had the opportunity to do but turned down because you were scared, didn't feel ready or were worried about what others would say. Perhaps you turned down the chance of love because you were afraid of getting hurt again, or others said it was too soon. Perhaps you had that great business idea but wrote it off because someone else was doing it or you didn't feel you had enough experience. Imagine for just one moment what could have been.

Some of the opportunities that have passed you by may pop up again, but most of them won't.

So, look back and feel that pain and regret and allow it to be a present day reminder that when new opportunities arise that you feel enthused about, you can't afford to pass them by?

What did you pass up or pass by that you wish you hadn't?

_____

_____

_____

_____

_____

_____

_____

_____

Why did you let that opportunity go?

What are your feelings about that now?

_____

_____

_____

_____

_____

_____

_____

_____

_____

_____

_____

_____

_____

_____

_____

_____

What would you now do differently?

_____

_____

_____

Pleased to hear it. There's too many great experiences you can have in life and now you won't let the next one pass you by because of fear.

I loved the movie *Sliding Doors* starring the beautiful Gwyneth Paltrow. It charts the two different lives and outcomes the main character would experience depending on if she missed her train or not.

With this idea in mind I want you to literally play out how your future could take two different paths depending on if you act on your dreams or not.

One future may be filled with regrets and disappointments and the other could be bursting with achievements, contentedness, fulfilment and gratitude. You're going to really step into those feelings so that you don't want to ever experience what's ahead down the negative path.

So, I want you to think about and visualise an area that most concerns you and how this area will continue to stall and digress if you choose to do nothing. How will things in this area look in time to come if you do jack shit and just expect them to get better by themselves?

What if you do nothing about your stable but stale relationship? What if you bury your head in the sand and don't deal with your debts? What if you do nothing about getting healthy? What if you do nothing about the job that you hate? What if you do nothing about that idea that is bubbling and burning inside of you? What if you never learn how to pull yourself up when you're down? Surely in time to come, things will just get slowly and progressively worse?

I want you to map out what is most likely to happen if you continue on your current course. What does life look like at each of these stages with no goals, no motivation and no kick-assery?

Three months from now: *e.g., I feel like I want to make changes but don't have the energy to do it right now.*

....

....

....

....

....

....

....

....

....

....

Six months from now: *e.g., I have really wanted to get started because I do feel sluggish and tired but I just don't have the time right now as it's a busy time of year for me.*

One year from now: *e.g., I've put on more weight instead of losing it. So, I not only feel disappointed in myself. I don't have the inclination to go out and have fun because I don't feel good. Life doesn't feel any better, in fact it feels much worse.*

Five years from now: *e.g., I feel tired and drained. Nothing seems to have gotten better. I don't enjoy my job and my friends' lives are much more fun and interesting than mine. The only hope I have to be happy is winning the lotto.*

....

....

....

....

....

....

....

....

....

....

....

....

....

....

Is this really how you want things to go down? Is that the way you want life to treat you? Well it will, unless you treat life with some respect and start to make the changes you want to see.

Now I want you to do this exercise again but this time we're going to lace it with your brilliance, smarts and sass.

So, imagine these same time periods in which you stepped up to life like the ultimate #girlboss. You smashed out your goals, you remained focused, you knew exactly what you wanted and no matter what bullshit got in your way you went out there and demanded it from the world. How different will life look when you achieve all this greatness?

Three months from now: *e.g., I've started my health improvement journey. I'm nervous but excited. I've made small adjustments and joined a gym/running club.*

Six months from now: *e.g., My new regime is habitual now. Things were slow to start but then the progress really started to show which has spurred me on even more. I feel amazing!*

One year from now: *e.g., I can't believe how much I have changed. My body and health have improved massively and that has boosted my confidence more than I could ever have imagined. I'm more inclined to try new things and experiences and I'm even going for an interview for a promotion that I would have never of thought I could have done a year ago.*

Five years from now: *e.g., WOW how life has changed. I'm in great relationship and I actually feel like I have a lot to give which I didn't years ago. I love my body confidence and I even feel sexy sometimes. Because I now set goals I make the things happen that are important to me. I really wanted to take some time out to travel which I did for two months last year and it was one of the best experiences of my life. I also wanted to make a slight change in my career path which I mapped out and achieved within 12 months. Life is good and I feel happy and that I am in control of what happens to me.*

Bejesus, that's more like it. You're a rock star in the making! I love that you're defining and designing your most glorious life. You deserve life to treat you better than good. You deserve life to be a blast, to be fun filled, to be outstanding, to live your truth and to reach the pinnacle goal of fulfilment. Can I get an amen?!

The truth is the doors are about to open onto the rest of your life and you've got the choice to stride down two very different paths. The first path will lead you to meagre mediocrity and the second path will lead you to a sense and presence of fulfilment that you never could have previously imagined. So, which path are you going to choose? Hopefully the latter, you know it's right and you know that's what you deserve.

I implore you to dump the fear and not allow your dreams to die with you. Strive for forward with everything you've got. Every day, people are getting older and passing away without having had the confidence to reveal their gifts and talents. Don't let that be you.

Share your ideas, products, services, time, compassion and energy because the impact you may have on someone else's life could be profound, you just don't know it yet. Without you stepping up to bat, so many people could be losing out on having you touch their lives and that quite frankly is out of order.

"Don't be selfish, share your good stuff."

If you are doubtful about whether or not you want to pursue something, ask yourself one of my favourite questions: 'What would my 80-year-old self say?'. I often get a very cheeky and sharp-witted response when I get my 80-year-old self to make a decision for me. She's quite rude and usually says something along the lines of: 'Oh for goodness sake, of course you can do that, and not only will you do it you'll love it and be brilliant too', bless her.

And you'll usually find that your 80-year-old self would have a similar thing to say and would much rather have had the experience, challenge, growth and learnings rather than passing the opportunity up. So go on, make your 80-year-old self, proud.

As you complete this last exercise I may just get a little soppy with you for a moment – I know – that's hard to believe. I hope and pray that you take some of the lessons, exercises, learnings, thoughts and ideas into your heart and use them not lose them, so you can create the reality that was truly destined for you. You know you can do this right? Throughout the process of completing this book you've already shown yourself that you can and I for one am pumped to see what is next for you.

You have clearly marked out the fork in your life's road and the path you now choose to take will be made with your decisions, actions and love or lack thereof, depending on what you want.

"Be a smartass and choose greatness, fulfilment and awesomeness for yourself."

Mind Your Health

"Take care of your body, it's the only place you have to live."

Jim Rohn

There is absolutely no point in kicking ass in the other areas of your life if you are going to neglect your health, because if you're neglecting your health, your biggest most valuable asset, the rest won't matter. You've only got one vehicle, so damn well look after it! What use is a shed load of cash if you're confined to a hospital bed with cancer – cancer doesn't accept cheques. What use is there meeting 'the one', starting to live out a real life love story only for them to watch you riddled with pain or discomfort? Why bother breaking through the glass ceiling only to crash back down to the floor with anxiety, burnout and depression?

When I think of my body, mind and soul, I think of it as a business. If you can learn to run your body like a business I'm certain you'll be successful. So, let's talk. How are you managing your business lately? Is it successful and thriving full of health and vigour? Is it just breaking even and hanging on by a thread? Or is it close to bankruptcy and you're just ignoring things.

To live your ideal life and do all of the amazing things you've written down in this book you need your health, strength, energy and vitality. If you want to fulfil that dream, start that enterprise, teach those kids, love with passion, travel and explore and you want to do it with zeal you need to have this health stuff like you need oxygen. And it isn't just about exercise and diet, although obviously they have huge parts to play. The quality of your sleep, your stress levels being low, your mind being calmed and relaxed are the essentials of health too.

Even if you're putting those life-changing things off for now, life is going to come at you hard and fast from all angles and you need to be as fit as a fiddle to duck and dive from its punches, otherwise it will knock you the fuck out. So, get up on your feet and create a health regime that works for you so that you can function at optimum. Don't be left huffing and puffing behind while your dreams take off without you and with someone else. Find your way to becoming an efficiently fuelled rock star. Play with your kids and be fit and able enough to join in. Be that someone who in retirement is freely travelling the world without the need for special assistance at the airport. Be that someone who didn't leave it to chance or fate, be that someone who loves and cherishes their body, because you know what, you're fucking worth it.

Look, I know that illness and disease can come knocking at your door from other external factors like genes, pollution, pesticides, the products we use on own our skin, but surely it's common sense to look after your body to the best of your ability? If you disagree that's fine you can cross your fingers and hope for the best. At least if you've taken care of yourself you've given yourself the best chance of experiencing great health.

Think about your current lifestyle. If you continued on your current path what will your old age most likely look like?

- Are you gaining weight year on year which will eventually become exponential?
- Are you making dietary decisions that could cause diabetes and high cholesterol?
- Are you feeding yourself with healthy food or junk food? And how does that food make you feel? Sluggish or bursting with energy?
- Are you consuming too much alcohol or drugs? How do you think that's affecting your body?
- Are you moving your body? And giving your body the chance to sweat and drain itself?

Our bodies were designed to move. Sign up for that Zumba or spin class, start swimming, cycling, hiking, rock climbing; try it out, whatever floats your boat just do it. If you don't like it, try something else until you find what form of exercise was made for you.

Also, if you don't already know, get to know how to fuel your body correctly. We live in an age where information is so easily available. So you don't have to go to the expense of studying a degree in nutrition, just buy a bloody book.

You've got one vehicle to carry you through this journey of life, don't fucking trash it on purpose!

Do your best and at least if something happens you'll have no regrets as you will know that you looked after yourself to the best of your ability. Everyday within your body are you are choosing to add a bit of poison and create disease, or you are giving your body the gift of nourishment? Learning to fuel myself rather than feed myself was an invaluable life lesson for me.

"Learn to fuel yourself not feed yourself."

Feeding is easy, fuelling takes smarts and discipline and builds health. Go for it!

Now look don't get me wrong, anyone who knows me knows that I love a glass or two (or, erm, five) of champagne, cava, prosecco, basically anything wet with bubbles. And I love savoury snacks like crisps or as some of you would say potato chips. Previously I could do a whole bag of Doritos in one sitting, no joke. But the thing is I don't eat and drink this shit all the time. This treat stuff isn't my regular stuff, it's my exceptional/on occasion stuff. I look forward to it and enjoy it but I mainly follow what I call the 80 / 20 rule. So I eat nutritionally 80% of the time and allow myself the treats I love 20% of the time. I know I'm loving my body and my body loves me right back. I know some people are like that sounds so boring, but honestly, I'll tell you what sounds boring to me – high cholesterol, blocked arteries and liver damage. Or feeling sluggish and lethargic, or being unhappy with a body that could change with good habits. None of that sounds like much fun to me so I'm going to do my best to avoid it all.

What you put in is what you'll get out, and what you get out is going to give you the energy and vibrancy to fulfil all of the things you want to achieve in the other areas of your life.

Describe your current state of health and fitness:

What can you do to improve it?
(*e.g., Drink less alcohol, start exercising, scheduling time to relax
and switch off.*)

What is the first step you can action within the next seven days to improve your health and fitness?
(e.g., Go to the trial class of salsa, buy some trainers for running, run a hot bath and enjoy it with no phone.)

_____

_____

_____

_____

_____

_____

_____

_____

_____

"I feel glorious dynamic energy. I am active and alive."

Louise Hay

Goodbye and God Bless

First, if you've read this far, huge congratulations!! You've managed to put up with me and my potty mouth and you've finished a nonfiction book, which is awesome, as I'm told about 60% of people don't finish the books they start to read. I sincerely hope you've enjoyed it and given yourself the gift of completing the exercises and finding out a lot more about yourself, your life and your future. If you skipped the exercises go back and do that shit right now, I mean seriously! This is life changing stuff for you.

If you've had any kind of breakthroughs, realisations, resolutions, ah ha moments, learnings, basically any good shit happening as a result of reading this, I really need to know about it. So get in touch with me and the team so we can give you a huge shout out, and more seriously I want to share these moments with the sisterhood that may be in a similar situation to you. Your story could be just the spark to ignite someone else's dream or help them through a difficult time so don't be shy come over and say 'Hi' and share your story with us at **nicolafindlay.com**.

I've often felt a little bit left at sea after I've finished a book, as in not sure what I should do next. You should have plenty of work to do from here to continue creating your dreams but if you think you might miss me which of course you will, and to tell you the truth I'm going to miss you too, feel free to come on over to **nicolafindlay.com** and sign up for my weekly video's, inspirations and bitchy rants and of course you can also follow me on Instagram and Facebook so that you can get your weekly diva dose of motivation.

Website: nicolafindlay.com
Facebook: Nicola Findlay The Coaching Diva
Insta: nicolafindlaytcd

So this doesn't have to be the end if you don't want it to be. I've still got your back.

Last Learning:
My biggest lesson learnt that I will savour, remember and utilise on a daily basis is:

....

....

....

Lastly I want you to know that whatever life throws at you:
You are loved
You are unique
You are special
You have a gift
You deserve your wildest dreams to come true

Sending Sexy, Huge, Kick Ass Hugs and Kisses
Ciao Bella, Coaching Diva Out xXx

Acknowledgements

Huge shout out and heartfelt thanks to Gareth and Hayley who turned my biggest dream into reality and made me a real life book whoop, whoop.

Nuff gratitude and love to the editing geniuses Peter and Claire who were able to make my ramblings and rants make sense to others not just me. No mean feat.

I'm so appreciative to my UK publicist Kate and her US partner in crime Josh for promoting this self-help book full of profanities. I'm sure having the F word in the title made their job lots of fun!

I've got to say thank you to Superstar Shaa Wasmund, she's got an MBE you know. My mentor and business hero.

And last but not least to my family and friends who supported me on this special journey – you know who y'all are.

END